DARK PSYCHOLOGY AND MANIPULATION

How to Improve Your Life. The Complete Beginner's Guide to Mind Control Techniques and Persuasion. Discover NLP Secrets and Learn How to Read People and Body Language

DANIEL BRAIN

© Copyright 2020 - All rights reserved.

TABLE OF CONTENTS

INTRODUCTION 6

CHAPTER 1: MANIPULATION AND DARK PSYCHOLOGY 10

WHAT IS DARK PSYCHOLOGY? 10
WHAT IS A MANIPULATIVE BEHAVIOR? 11
CAUSES OF MANIPULATIVE BEHAVIORS 12
EXAMPLES OF MANIPULATIVE BEHAVIORS 13

CHAPTER 2: MAIN TYPES OF MANIPULATION (EXAMPLES OF MANIPULATION AND HOW TO APPLY THEM) 16

COVERT EMOTIONAL MANIPULATION 17
MANIPULATION IN THE WORKPLACE 21

CHAPTER 3: HOW PSYCHOLOGY IS USED TO MANIPULATE AND INFLUENCE PEOPLE IN THEIR DAILY LIVES 22

MANIPULATION IN OUR DAILY LIVES 25

CHAPTER 4: THE EFFECT ON PEOPLE 36

CHAPTER 5: HOW TO UNDERSTAND IF OTHERS ARE MANIPULATING YOU 46

HOW TO IDENTIFY AND DETECT MANIPULATIVE PEOPLE 46
WHY DO PEOPLE MANIPULATE? 50
MANIPULATION IS ABOUT FEAR AND UNWORTHINESS 52
MANIPULATION IS ABOUT LACK OF CONSCIOUSNESS 53
COMMUNICATION 57
INDEED MEANS MAYBE 58
THE CHILD WITHIN 59

CHAPTER 6: HOW TO UNDERSTAND IF PEOPLE WANT TO MANIPULATE US AND RECOGNIZE PERSUASION TECHNIQUES 60

UNDERSTANDING DARK PERSUASION 61
UNMASKING THE DARK PERSUADER 63
DARK PERSUASION TECHNIQUES TO BE ON THE LOOKOUT FOR 65

CHAPTER 7: HOW TO UNDERSTAND AND MANAGE EMOTIONS AND THOSE OF OTHERS 74

UNDERSTANDING YOUR EMOTIONS 74
THE DISADVANTAGES OF YOUR EMOTIONS 85
THE BENEFITS OF YOUR EMOTIONS 88
RESPONSE VERSUS REACTION 89
EMOTIONAL MANIPULATION 92

CHAPTER 8: WHAT TO DO AND HOW TO BEHAVE IF PEOPLE WANT TO MANIPULATE US **96**

HOW TO APPLY THESE TECHNIQUES AGAINST A MANIPULATOR 98
KNOW WHAT YOU WANT AND HOW YOU FEEL......................................99
STAND YOUR GROUND 100
BE PREPARED FOR BACKLASH...100
CUT THEM OFF.. 101

CHAPTER 9: HOW NOT TO BE MANIPULATED **107**

HOW TO DEFEND YOURSELF FROM MANIPULATORS.............................. 107
ACT FAST 109
GET ASSISTANCE QUICKLY 110
HAVE CONFIDENCE IN YOUR INSTINCTS..112

CHAPTER 10: BEHAVIORAL TRAITS OF FAVORITE VICTIMS OF MANIPULATORS **115**

EMOTIONAL INSECURITY AND FRAGILITY 116
SENSITIVE PEOPLE 118
EMPATHIC PEOPLE...119
FEAR OF LONELINESS..121
FEAR OF DISAPPOINTING OTHERS 123
PERSONALITY DEPENDENT DISORDERS AND EMOTIONAL DEPENDENCY 124

CHAPTER 11: HOW TO READ AND ANALYZE PEOPLE **127**

HOW TO READ PEOPLE... 127
ESTABLISH A BASELINE...128
HOW TO ANALYZE PEOPLE 130

CHAPTER 12: MICRO EXPRESSIONS AND BODY LANGUAGE – A BASIC PRIMER...**135**

NONVERBAL CUES ASSOCIATED WITH SITTING...................................138
NONVERBAL CUES ASSOCIATED WITH ARMS......................................139
NONVERBAL EXPRESSIONS ASSOCIATED WITH FINGERS AND HAND
GESTURES...140
NONVERBAL GESTURES OF THE HEAD 143
MISCELLANEOUS NONVERBAL CUES 144
GENERAL PSYCHOLOGICAL FRAMEWORK...149
THE DARK CONTINUUM 150
THE DARK FACTOR..151
THE DARK SINGULARITY 154

CONCLUSION **159**

5

Introduction

Among the fundamental human rights is the freedom for every living being to have opinions, points of view, perception, and perhaps a say to every matter that arises. Forcefully taking away this right from individuals is an unfair and inhuman act, and is therefore against the law in many nations of the world. But then, people still tamper with others' perceptions, manipulate people's minds for diverse reasons without applying force. This is called "The Psychological Manipulation" and of course, not a crime.

The ability to manipulate minds is indeed a great gift, skill, and a great possession to any and every human. In fact, it is fun to manipulate minds but not in any way funny to be manipulated. As the manipulated, you may feel emotionally bullied, you may sense cheating, or develop a kind of inferiority complex towards the manipulator, You don't have to negate this psychological skill and art of manipulation, all you need to do is to be on a safer side by learning about the art of manipulation.

Not only the power embedded in the possession of the skill, but the results to be gotten from the effective utilization of this gift is enough to paint psychological manipulation as one thing that a goal-oriented and smart person must possess. Psychological manipulation is basically about getting into people's subconscious, reading minds, getting people to do what you want them to do (believing you, performing an action, making or taking a decision, accepting your stand on an argument, confessing, obeying an authority, following an instruction...). In this case, not with force but by convincing them and making them see the reason to do what you need them to do. It is basically being smart psychologically and using it to achieve your aim. It is your ability to study, persuade, influence and manipulate minds and get people to be on your side irrespective of their initial stand or characteristic. With this said so far, it'll be pertinent to present a detailed, relatable and realistic example of how manipulation works.

There was a time when one of my cousins would always get me to agree with him on whatever we were discussing or arguing about. He was so good that I couldn't win an argument even with my clearly valid points that were better than his. What I know he had was that he knew how to make me agree with him. Even when I tried to prove smart, he was apparently smarter. He could control my mind through persuasion and not force. Like magic, he would always know what I was thinking about, hence, he could easily counter my thoughts and propositions. He had studied me well and his psychological manipulation was prime. But as time went on, I got to realize that being able to get people to reason with you, be on your side, change their perceptions or get yours to fit with theirs, win arguments, get into their minds isn't magic after all. It was and still is a matter of being smart and using your smartness to its fullest capacity - psychological manipulation.

Studying people, reading minds, observing people and situations, taking advantage of circumstances, watching more and talking less, doing lots of critical thinking are other ways of getting to be a controller of minds, a psychological manipulator, and a very persuasive and influential individual.

Does any idea of manipulation come lurking in your head yet? Are you able to visualize any incidence or a potential incidence of manipulation you've ever come across? Do you feel so elated now because you've realized that you have subconsciously used the psychological manipulation power on someone before? Or you fall into the "I don't even have any idea of what you're saying" category? Worry not, whatever category you are, this book is here for you but before we move into the business, let's create a little image.

Another relatable example or experience we might have had with manipulation is the manipulation that is contained in the power of persuasion through brand's PR (Public Relation) officers and marketers while they provide you with messages that capture your attention, sustain your interest, create impressions on you and sometimes even influence your perceptions and or purchase decisions. Persuasion and manipulation happen even on the streets; getting to be convinced by a saleswoman at the nearby grocery store about patronizing her store. Another example is when your mom would buy you a storybook then instead of a toy, and was able to convince you to understand why you needed the book and not the toy. It is used by a cheating lover when he tries to erase his cheating record from your mind and slowly drift the blame away from himself and unto you. Can you relate it to those your neighbors, who are persistently encouraging and persuading you to come to their social or cultural group? When you're influenced and convinced into visiting the library every day or drinking every other day because you've been conditioned to do so owing to the manipulative abilities of your peer. So you see that the "playing with minds" and the persuasion thing is a chain with endless rings. Would you keep being the manipulated?

I doubt your answer is yes. This is the book made for you to read with all the concentration and interest in the world. You've likely grabbed a copy though for you to be seeing this however, there's one more thing, read up! Soon enough, you will learn to control minds and have the necessary persuasive effects of a good mind controller. While getting an insight into what this book is all about, you'll get to understand that manipulation is not evil after all, it's a rather effective use of smartness, sound intellect, and persuasive abilities. Read on!

CHAPTER 1:

Manipulation And Dark Psychology

What Is Dark Psychology?

Dark Psychology is the art of manipulation and the control of one's mind. The dark triad (or the Dark triad) is a personality profile, based on a combination of the following factors:

Psychopathy (Psychopathy): This is an attribute of a person or persons with a tough personality, "callous," cruel behaviors, and a very limited empathy. They are people who have no remorse, no morals, and no ethical standards, are indifferent, and are often cynical and insensitive.

Machiavellianism (Machiavellianism): This consists of people with superficial charm and very manipulative behaviors. For instance, these are people who can use other people to get what they want; they lie, they take advantage of who they can cheat on and cheat.

Narcissism (Narcissism): This consists of beliefs of superiority, grandiosity, vanity, and high emotional explosiveness. They are people who want everyone to admire them and pay attention to them, who believe they deserve a higher status or a social prestige and expect special and favorable treatment, who, if they are not treated as they think they deserve, can react with anger, rage or aggressiveness.

Also, they are usually people with an unpleasant treatment (even being superficially charming), with very limited self-control (they can be very nice and suddenly have a fit of anger); they are usually aggressive, not very responsible and are not honest. There is a great difference between the sexes, because it is much more frequent to find this personality profile in men than in women, unlike other personality profiles (such as an anxious profile).

What Is A Manipulative Behavior?

Deception is the center of a manipulative behavior. Very manipulative people are experts in the game of deception and in combination with the general coldness that they (often) have, they are merciless. People who manipulate a lot often do not see people as living beings, but rather as a means to reach a goal.

That often means that once they have arrived at their 'destination,' they will certainly not think twice about leaving you on the side of the road. The worst part is that they sometimes want to play it so that you are the guilty one and they are the victim. That is the tricky thing with people with manipulative behaviors. Their characteristics range from small things like insisting that you come to their office or taking you by surprise and a host of other things. This is also in line with one of the other important parts of manipulative behaviors; intimidation. Manipulators like to intimidate and belittle because it puts them in their position of power and puts them above others.

People manipulate for the sake of power, money, status and vanity. So manipulation is often the improvement of one's situation (at the expense of others!)

Causes Of Manipulative Behaviors

Unfortunately, the cliché that people who show manipulative behaviors during their youth have been mistreated or have suffered trauma, is true.

Being physically or emotionally abused by narcissistic parents for instance, can have a huge effect on a child who can end up expressing himself in terribly nasty ways.

Another reason that people behave manipulatively is when there is a lot at stake, such as in politics.

A certain class of people will do everything to stay in power once they have experienced it, with all the consequences that entail.

Many narcissistic people, such as managers and politicians, do everything to maintain their power and status.

This is also why a 'ladder' is created at schools and universities with a group of people who will do everything to stay 'at the top.'

The parties, luxury houses and cars, expensive watches, and designer clothing, everything is about them to convey a sense of authority. Often times, these people are also narcissists.

However, there are also people who naturally have the impulse to behave manipulatively, and they are often found in some of the situations mentioned above. These people are also called psychopaths.

Examples Of Manipulative Behaviors

Although this may all sound a bit far away and perhaps even unrealistic, manipulative behaviors are found in our daily lives. For instance, you wrote an important file yesterday afternoon and gave it to a colleague so that he could look at it again and then send it back to you but when you came to work this morning, your boss was at your desk and started screaming angrily at you saying that you never wrote that file.

So after your boss was done shouting, finished, you went on high legs to your colleague, and something very strange happened; your colleague claimed that you never gave him that file, but he did it in such a convincing way that you began to doubt your memory!

This is gas lighting and is a textbook example of manipulative behavior.

Manipulative people will also not accept guilt under any circumstances; for instance,

Your friend and you fought this week, and after thinking about it for a while, you concluded that your reactions were a bit exaggerated.

So you determine to go to your friend's house to make it up, and after you had apologized and it got accepted, you noticed that your friend did not apologize.

If you asked for it subtly, the answer would be short: "No, of course, I don't have to apologize! If you hadn't done something that stupid, I wouldn't have gotten angry. "

This is, of course is strange reasoning and is almost iconic for manipulative behaviors.

Another good example of manipulative a behavior is for instance, you fell ill this week and it was so bad that even walking from the bed to the couch was too much trouble.

One week later you felt a little better. Later on, you decided to go encourage your son to play football and you happen to tell one of the parents that you could not take your son for the match because you were ill. The answer you got was not what you expected:

"Is that all? That's nothing, man! Last year I was so sick that I bruised my lungs, I coughed so hard yet I stood along the line but because you have to be there for your children, you had to come along. You are a good parent, aren't you? "

Not only was this a bad answer (because you were sick last week and you really couldn't), it was also a manipulative answer.

The parent had not only minimized your problems and put them in the spotlight, he also belittled you.

CHAPTER 2:

Main Types Of Manipulation (Examples Of Manipulation and How To Apply Them)

There are several types of manipulation because it can often depend on where the manipulator is or who they are manipulating. For example, there are some manipulators who focus on workplace tactics and there are manipulators, who will use their tactics no matter where they are or who they are with.

Covert Emotional Manipulation

Covert emotional manipulation is a part of any form of manipulation. However, it is stronger in people who are known as "master manipulators" or people who will manipulate anyone in order to get anything they want. It is not as strong as a manipulation tactics people use when they tell someone they are fine, even when something is wrong.

At the base of this manipulation, the aim is to change the way people feel and think, which is referred to as covert emotional manipulation. They focus on your conscious awareness in order to control you. Because of this, people don't often realize that they are being manipulated.

First, the manipulator will get you to trust them. Then, they will start to control the way you feel, think, and perceive situations. This will happen slowly as they don't want you to catch on to the manipulation. Once they feel that your emotions and thoughts are in their hands, they will start to tear apart your confidence. A master manipulator knows they have to lower your self-esteem in order to control you the way they want to. They will also work to take away your identity, which allows you to fully become theirs.

While they are trying to break you down emotionally and mentally, they will also try to keep you away from your family and friends. One of the biggest reasons for this is to prevent people who knew you before they came into your life from coming to you because they see them as a threat. Your family and friends will notice a change in you, and they won't like it. They will try to find out why you are changing and, typically very quickly, they point their fingers at the manipulator. When this happens, your friends and family will do what they can to try to see what this person is doing to you and how you are being treated. This is one of the most common signs of manipulation in relationships.

Of course, you will start to notice a change within yourself. Unfortunately, it is usually after the manipulator has had control over you. You start to notice yourself change when you begin to feel different. You might notice you have anxiety, you are depressed, having trouble sleeping, you struggle trusting people you once trusted, and you become increasingly isolated ("Covert Emotional Manipulation").

For most people, it is hard to spot the signs of manipulators. This is especially true for people who suffer from manipulation from their significant other. In general, it is hard to spot certain signs of manipulation. Furthermore, it is often harder to spot these behaviors from people who you love and believe love you back. In relationships, people often turn a "blind eye" to their significant other's manipulative ways because they see them as faults. We work to understand the faults of each other in relationships.

While you will want to notice the personality traits of a manipulator, there are a lot of other signs when it comes to manipulation in relationships. This is because manipulators often let down their guard a bit when they are at home. They are in their comfort zone and believe they can do anything, and you won't protect yourself or try to change it because you are too weak.

1. They will start a fight with you over something minor.

Manipulators need to win, and this is frequently displayed in their relationships, especially romantic relationships. Therefore, you may notice that if you are having a minor disagreement with your significant other, they will turn it into a fight so that you allow them to win. They want you to give up and do whatever they want to done.

2. They are great secret keepers.

While they don't like it when you keep any secret from them, they can keep anything they want from you. Furthermore, they don't have to tell you anything they are doing or where they are going. This simply doesn't matter to you. In other words, what they do is their business and you need to mind your own.

However, if you treat them the same way, they will start a fight, tell you that you don't love them, or become angry. This is because if they don't know everything about you, they are losing their control. They are also able to keep control away from you by not letting you know their secrets.

3. Their actions and words don't match.

Manipulators realize that in order to keep you in their control, they need to sometimes give you what you want. While this can come in the form of gifts, they will usually focus on telling you what you want to hear. However, they will not follow through with their words. For example, if you are feeling lonely and don't want your significant other to go out with their friends again, you will ask them to stay with you. You will ask for time alone or to go with them. They will give you an excuse for why tonight won't work, but then make a promise to spend more time with you or both of you will do something another night. Unfortunately, they will rarely follow through with their promise.

4. They will act like the victim.

There is always a time that you are going to argue with your significant other or try to stand up for yourself. This not only happens in the beginning but throughout the relationship. When it does, the manipulator is going to play the role of the victim. They will twist your words to make it seem like you are the one who is doing something wrong. While you might not agree with this perception at first, they will continue to use their emotions to persuade you to believe them.

Manipulation in the Workplace

Many people deal with workplace manipulation at some point in their career. Sometimes it is because one of their co-workers is a manipulator while other times it is everyday forms of manipulation. For example, a co-worker manipulates you into helping them with their task or gets you to do their task. They only do this because they don't like this specific responsibility. Sometimes you will start to notice your supervisor is a manipulator. Unfortunately, this is highly common in the workplace as many supervisors have used manipulation to get their position, especially if they worked themselves up the ladder. However, you should never assume your supervisor is manipulative. If they are, they will typically demonstrate signs of being a manipulator, such as bullying, blaming others, making their staff look guilty, giving their staff the silent treatment, and distorting facts. One way to know if you're working with a manipulator is by the way you are treated. Manipulators need to make sure you know your place, meaning you are beneath them. Therefore, they will often make sarcastic comments that make you feel inferior. For example, you come to work one day in professional attire that is more casual than your company usually wears. Instead of a white shirt and a suit, you decide to wear a white shirt with slacks. When your co-worker notices your attire, they start to belittle your clothes, making fun of your low income and how you can't afford nicer clothes because of that.

CHAPTER 3:

How Psychology Is Used To Manipulate And Influence People In Their Daily Lives

People use psychology within their daily lives, so why not use Dark Psychology and the tactics to protect yourself in your everyday life. There are quite a few personality traits that can be very harmful if you get caught up in them. Sadists fall under this category. For instance, this personality type enjoys inflicting suffering on others, especially those who are innocent. They will even do this at their own risk. Those who are diagnosed as sadists feel that cruelty is a type of pleasure, which to them is exciting, and can even be sexually stimulating.

We do have to face the fact that we manipulate people and deceive people all the time. When it comes to deception, people not only deceive others on a daily basis, they also deceive themselves too. People often lie to gain something or to avoid something. They might not want to be punished for an action, or they might want to reach a goal, and they self-deceive to get there.

Here are some examples of how people can deceive themselves:

Having a hard time studying: This is a common occurrence. For instance this occurs with people who desire to study, yet they get distracted by so many things, especially cell phones and social media apps. They can also find just about anything to distract them from the task at hand. These types of people seem to have a phobia for studying long or well enough and they are afraid that they will come home with a bad grade and it will show how unintelligent they are. So, they take the art of self-deception and come up with the idea that will help prevent them from studying. This excuse will weigh better in their minds if they do end up getting a bad grade on their test.

The person's subconscious is telling them that it is better for them to get bad grades for lack of studying than to study and fail and thus get blamed for their unintelligence.

They certainly can't live with that.

Here are other ways that we regularly deceive ourselves:

- Procrastinating – People often waste time when they do not want to study or do something important. However, the main reason for procrastinating could be the phobia of failing and procrastinating was just an excuse. Self-confidence can be an issue as well.

- Drinking, doing drugs and carrying out bad habits - People often fall into bad habits like drinking, or doing drugs just to have something to blame if they fail more than once. This type of person will try to convince himself/herself that if they could stop doing drugs, they could be very successful. When they are the ones deceiving themselves and standing in their own way.

- People often hold back because life is unfair. They tell themselves that we all live in a big lie that most people believe in, but not them. It is easier to blame it on life being unfair, than hold themselves accountable for not reaching their goals.

If you realize that you have been deceiving yourself, here are a couple of things that you can do to change that.

- Remember that you are smart and the fact that you have been able to deceive yourself reaffirms it. If you were not smart, there would have been no way that you would have been able to come up with some of those ideas.

- It is important to learn how to face your fears. If you are running from a certain trauma, or not wanting to take a test, you have to remind yourself that you are stronger than this and that you can beat it.

- Lastly, once you face your fears, your self-confidence and courage will grow.

Manipulation In Our Daily Lives

Manipulation is an underhanded tactic that we are exposed to on a daily basis. Manipulators are people who want nothing more than to get their needs met, but they will use shady methods to do so.

Those who grew up being manipulated, or were around manipulation, find it hard to determine what is really going on because if you are experiencing it again, it might feel familiar. Maybe you were manipulated in a previous relationship, or the current relationship that you are in reminds you of your childhood.

This is important because manipulation tactics break apart communication and breaks a person's trust. People will often find ways to manipulate the situation and play games rather than speaking honestly about what is going on. However, others value communication only to manipulate the situation to reveal the weaknesses of the other person, so that they can be in control. These types of people do this often in conversation. They have no concern with listening to others talk about themselves and they are not there to help those people get through whatever it is that they are going through. It is all about dominance in this case and that's it.

Here are some of the tactics that can be used on an everyday basis:

Some of the common techniques that we can experience are:

- Lying – White lies, untruths, partial or half-truths, exaggerations, and stretching the truth.

- Love Flooding – Through endless compliments, affection or through what is known as buttering someone up.

- Love Denial – telling someone that they do not love you and withholding your love or affection from them until you get what you want.

- Withdrawal – through avoiding the person altogether or giving them the silent treatment.

- Choice Restriction – Giving people options that distract them from the one decision that you don't want them to make.

- Reverse Psychology – Trying to get a person to do the exact opposite of what you want them to do in the attempt to motivate them to do the direct opposite, which is what you really wanted them to do in the first place.

- Being Condescendingly Sarcastic or Having a Patronizing Tone – To be fair, we are all guilty of doing this once in a while. But those who manipulating in conversations are doing this consistently. They are mocking you, their tone sounding as if you are a child, and they belittle you with their words.

- Speaking in Universal Statement or Generalizations – The manipulator will take the statement and make it untrue by grossly making it bigger. Generalizations are afforded to those who a part of a group of things. A universal statement is more personal.

  → Example: Universal Example: You always say things like that.

→ Example: Generalization: Therapists always act like that.

- Luring and Then Playing Innocent – We, or someone we know, is good at pushing the buttons of our loved ones. However, when a manipulator tries to push the buttons of their spouse and then act like they have no idea what happened. They automatically get the reaction that they were after and this is when their partner needs to pay close attention to what they are doing. Those who are abusive will keep doing this again and again until their spouse will start wondering if they are crazy.

- Bullying - This is one of the easiest forms of manipulation to recognize. For example, your spouse asks you to clean the kitchen. You don't want to, but the look they give you indicates that you'd better cleaned it or else. You tell them you'd clean, but this was because they had just used a form of violence to get you to do what they wanted. Later they could have told you that you could have said no, but you knew you couldn't. It is important to note that if you fear that you cannot say no in your relationship without fearing for your safety, then you need to leave the relationship.

- Using Your Heart Against You – Your spouse finds a stray kitten and wants to bring it home. The logical thing to do would be to discuss being able to house and afford the cat. But instead, they take the manipulative approach. Their ultimate goal is to make you feel bad about not being able to take care of the animal. Don't let anyone, even your spouse, make you feel that you cannot make the best choice for you. You do not have to take care of the kitten if you don't want to. Bottom line, meet their manipulations with reasonable alternatives.

- "If you love me, you would do this" –This one is so hard because it challenges how you feel about your spouse. They are asking you to prove your love for them by giving them what they want from you, making you feel guilt and shame. All you can do in this situation is to stop it altogether. You can tell your spouse that you love them without having to go to the store. If they wanted you to go, they could just ask.

- Emotional Blackmail – This is ugly and dangerous. The idea that someone will harm themselves if you leave them is harmful at the core. They are using guilt, fear, and shame to keep having power over you. Remember that no one's total well-being is completely your responsibility. You have to tell yourself not to fall for it. This will always be a manipulation tactic. However, you can tell them that if they are feeling like they are going to harm themselves that you will call an ambulance to help them.

- Neediness when it's Convenient – Has your spouse started to feel sick or upset when they didn't get what they wanted? This is a direct form of manipulation. For instance, they don't want to go somewhere with you and suddenly develop a panic attack which you'd have to help them through so that they don't get to go at all. This is not healthy at all, and if this persists, you should think about ending the relationship.

- They Are Calm in Bad Situations – When someone gets hurt or somebody dies, your spouse always seem to not react with any feeling. They are always calm. This type of manipulation makes one think that perhaps how they are reacting is a bit much or maybe their emotions are a little bit out of control. This is a controlling mechanism because no one should be able to tell you how to feel. This might seem like they are questioning your mental health and maturity level and you find yourself looking to them on and how to respond to certain situations. If this is something that happens often and you see that you keep falling for it, you might need to go and see a therapist. This way, they can help you work on your emotional responses and find your true feelings again.

This manipulation method can be very damaging to your psyche. At the moment, learn to trust your gut. It will not steer you wrong.

- Everything is a Joke – This is a two-part manipulation tactic. Your spouse will say hurtful things about you, and then when you get upset, they get upset because you can't take a joke. At other times, they will joke about you in front of others, and if you don't respond positively, you are again ruining the fun. This is a way to put you down continuously without having to take responsibility for it. Remember that you are not ruining the fun here, but you have to stand up for yourself.

- Forcing Their Insecurities On To You – Here, your spouse for instance, will manipulate you into thinking that their insecurities are now your problem and will use them in a way to control you. They will tell you that they have been cheated on before, and that's why they wouldn't like you to keep male friends and that you should stop. Or they use them when they act a certain way, controlling your behavior because they don't want to lose you. When it comes to this situation, you have to find a balance. You can care for someone and make sure that you are considerate of their feelings, but you should not be manipulated into feeling what your spouse wants you to feel. Their manipulation is ruled by guilt.

- Makes You Responsible and Accountable for What He/She Feels – This manipulation tactic is quite funny because your spouse spends a great deal of time making you think and feel like you cannot think about your or their feelings on your own, but that you have to be reminded of how they feel. They tell you how you feel, and that you are responsible for how they feel. If they're sad, you made them sad. You must have done something to make them feel that way. This tactic belittles you also because they take a lot from you and tell you how you feel, but then they want you to be responsible for how they feel.

- Makes You Want What They Want, and Makes You Believe That Too – We all make compromises in relationships. However, what is not normal is having to put aside what you want completely to appease your spouse so that you can fully commit to what they want. If you soon start to see that your spouses' needs are being met far more often than yours, you need to start questioning things. You need to ask yourself if you are giving them what they want because you want to, or because they made you feel guilty or a sense of irresponsibility for how they feel. If you find that you are giving up everything for them, then you need to reconsider what is actually important.

When determining how to get away from those who manipulate you, it is important to know your fundamental human rights and how you should not be treated.

You have the right:

- To be respected and treated with respect.

- To express how you feel, your opinions and the things you want and need.

- To set your own priorities and goals.

- To say no and not feel guilty about it.

- To get what you pay for without guilt or shame.

- To have an opinion that is different from those in the group.

- To stand up for yourself.

- To take care of yourself.

- To protect yourself from being threatened or harmed psychically, mentally and emotionally.

- And, to create your own life full of happiness.

These specific rights help you set important boundaries that will help protect you in the future. We do have to remember that there will be people in this world who do not respect these rights or us as people, but see us as just things they can use to move on to the next phase. Do not let others take you over and manipulate your life. You are the only one who has power and authority over your life. And you are the only one who is in charge of it too.

Keep your distance from those who you think are trying to manipulate you or others. See how they act when they are around different people in different situations.

Avoid blaming yourself, even though it is common to feel that way when someone is trying to expose your weaknesses and use them for their personal gain. You have to keep telling yourself that you are not the problem and that they are trying to get you to surrender your power. If this occurs, ask some very basic questions: is my spouse treating me with respect? Are they reasonable with me? Do I feel good about myself while in the relationship? And, finally, is this relationship going two ways or one?

35

CHAPTER 4:

The Effect On People

The idea behind being a persuasive person which is the main objective of persuasion is to get something in return. There is no sense in practicing the art of persuasion, if there is nothing desired in return. Persuasion means to cause someone to do something specific. Therefore, some sort of gain is desired, some sort of end result.

In order to know the intended end result of the persuasive effort, there must be a defined desired outcome. The person doing the persuading wants something tangible, something definable. But what do they want? Well, that is completely up to them to decide which often happens before they engage in any form of persuasion which is exactly what they hope to achieve at the end of the conversation.

This is what is meant as defining desired outcomes. The thing that is desired must be decided before any kind of persuasive tactics begin so that the person doing the persuading understands the desired outcome.

For instance, the staff of a particular office decides to hold a meeting to decide the location of a new office because the old office seems small and cramped and business is growing and thus needs more room to be able to continue its grow. So an office meeting will take place where the new location will be decided upon. This is the first step in defining the desired outcome, knowing what the proposed outcome is. In this case, it is the location of the new office.

So the meeting has been set for a particular time and place. Finished, right? Wrong! Without some sort of order and organization, the meeting will be unproductive and the desired outcome probably will not happen. The meeting is crucial to the desired outcome. Without some sort of specific plan then the meeting is nothing more than people in an office meeting in one room to make conversation.

So now it is necessary to set up the meeting; to have a plan as to how the meeting will proceed. Since this is a meeting that involves the entire office staff, there might not be any need to decide who to invite since everyone would be in attendance. So, the next step would be to create the agenda for the meeting; Will there be time for questions? Will certain people be invited to participate by offering specific recommendations for the new location? How will the ultimate decision be reached? All these factors need to be decided before the meeting begins.

When beginning the meeting be sure to mention the desired outcome. Let everyone know exactly what they are there to discuss. Make sure everyone involved knows and understand the desired outcome. Set a specific time for discussion and a time when the decision will be made. Then when the meeting is reaching the end of its prescribed time, restate the objective and determine if a decision can be made or if more research is needed.

An outcome is nothing more than an end result that can be seen and measured. It is the consequence of the action. It is the conclusion that comes from persuading someone to do something. In any desired outcome, there are four things that will need to be decided before the desired outcome can be decided upon. Those four things are; is the desire for something specific there? Is something already owned needing to be kept? Who should be connected with and how? what skills are needed to achieve the desired outcome?

It is important to decide these things because the underlying objectives will definitely affect the way the outcome is to be gained. It is similar to a football game where there is a defensive team and an offensive team. One group attacks the opposing team and one group defends against the attacks from the opposing teams. Each team will have a different set of priorities and procedures. Their desired outcomes will be quite different from one another. Each team will need to decide what it is they want to learn, defend, or acquire. The goal will determine the game plan.

Some sort of change needed has been identified and will be achieved. The path to achievement begins with setting a goal. The end of this journey is the desired outcome. It is necessary to understand that these are two separate entities that work together to achieve a result.

A goal is a destination. An outcome is a specific thing; it can be seen and measured. While setting the goal is vital to receiving the outcome, they are two very different things and should be treated as such.

Goals always have reasons behind them. Something that is thought of as being necessary to happiness, to wealth, to health, or just because it is truly desired, is just not there. Whatever the reason is, it is that exact reason that drives forward progress toward the desired outcome. In order to be able to progress, to go forward to the goal, that goal and the idea of achieving it must be firmly entrenched in your mind. Without a steady focus on the goal, there is no possibility that the goal will ever be reached.

Imagine going to work every day for fifteen years, doing the same job every day. Imagine this is a job that needed college courses, so it was a chosen job. During the past fifteen years, doing the same job every day has been rewarding and profitable. There have been several promotions, the last of which came with a private secretary and a lovely large office. Several other people, who have not been working here quite as long, are now the team that directly reports to you every Monday in this large new office.

But all of a sudden, going to work becomes somewhat boring. The job just does not bring the amount of satisfaction it once did. The problem is not in the job itself but in the person doing the job. What seemed so right all those years now feels so wrong. What is really desired her, is more interaction with people. In managing other people, a new skill has to emerged which is the ability to take raw recruits and mold them into productive team members with a bright future. That is the job that brings happiness and satisfaction.

But while this thought has been firmly entrenched in the mind for months now, no changes have been made to get closer to the goal of that type of occupation and so every Monday morning is filled with team meetings, every day is filled with spreadsheets, and every Friday is filled with boundless joy that another work week has passed. Why?

The answer to that is procrastination. Whether intentional or unintentional, procrastination has ruined many good intentions. Unintentional procrastination does happen sometimes. Everyone has that moment of "oops! I meant to take care of that today I'll get to it first thing in the morning." That is unintentional; something was forgotten. Intentional procrastination means knowing something needs to be done but putting it off until whenever. Many people do this with dreams and desires, especially those that will require extra work to accomplish or simply just a big leap of faith. Changing careers when one is firmly established is a scary thing. But what someone wants at twenty is not necessarily what they'd want at forty. People change. Their hearts change. They must be willing to follow their dreams and make them a reality. But people procrastinate out of fear.

So ask these three questions:

- What exactly am I afraid of? Do I fear to lose a great job that will pay for my kid's college because I may not be able to find one that pays as well? What if I have to take a pay cut and can no longer pay the mortgage? What happens if I lose my health insurance? These are all valid question that must be addressed when considering a large change in employment.

- What will I gain if I am able to conquer this fear? What great gain will be realized? Will it be a new job, a new career that is more in line with current life goals? Maybe the real dream is the chance to help other people.

- What do I do to fight this fear? Accept the fear as real. Acknowledge its existence. Then make a plan to reach the new goal and proceed without waiting. Go forward without procrastination.

Now, it is time to set a goal to make this dream a reality. Identify the goal as specifically. The more specific the goal, the better the chance is to realize that goal. Vague goals are nothing more than wishes. It is as simple as the difference between "I want to lose weight" and "I want to lose twenty pounds." The second statement is a specific goal that can be measured, as work towards it progresses.

Know exactly what is desired as a reward when the goal is achieved. If the goal is weight loss, perhaps the reward is being able to wear that dress featured in the store window. If the goal is learning how to swim, then maybe the goal is to swim in the ocean for the first time ever. Plan how this goal will be achieved. Think about the senses that will be used along the way and how they will make this progress easier or more difficult.

Visualize the plan and try to imagine any possible obstacles. That does not mean putting the obstacles in the path, but in being aware of the possibility that they might crop up and having a plan to defeat them. If the intended goal involves weight loss, what will be the plan for coping with the buffet during the holiday season? If the goal is to complete classes online, then what happens if the internet goes out or the computer crashes? It is necessary to have a back-up plan to deal with life's little emergencies.

What will be used for markers along the way to track progress toward the goal? If the goal is weight loss, then perhaps a wall chart with every five pounds lost marked in red. Perhaps a drawing of a thermometer, with the goal being the mercury bulb at the top, and the thermometer is filled in gradually with every pound lost. Have a system in place to track these milestones.

Be aware that working toward any goal might come with negatives attached. Changing careers will most certainly mean a change in income. What if the career change means moving to another state? Is that a viable option? An extreme amount of weight loss will mean constantly refreshing the wardrobe. It is important to be aware of anything that might be seen as a negative effect of reaching the goal. These must be acceptable or the goal will need to be changed.

And when little distractions occur along the way, do not let them cancel out any progress that has already been made. Life happens. All roads have bumps in them. Even Shakespeare knew that no matter how good the plan was, it might not work. So acknowledge the fact that little bumps in the road will happen and have a plan to overcome them. Maybe it was a temporary lapse in judgment or it is a sign that the current path needs to take a bit of a different direction. The choice is solely up to the person who set the goal and created the path. And when the goal is reached, so will be the desired outcome.

45

CHAPTER 5:

How To Understand If Others Are Manipulating You

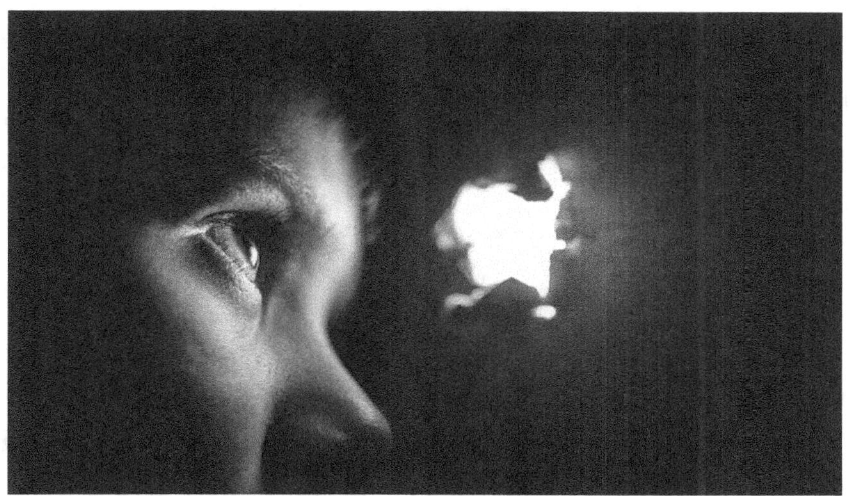

How To Identify And Detect Manipulative People

If you've at any point felt like something is off in a cozy relationship or have an easygoing experience or you feel you're being forced, controlled, or even feel like you're addressing yourself more than expected—it could be manipulation.

"Manipulation is a genuinely undesirable mental strategy utilized by people who are unequipped for requesting what they need, in an immediate manner. "People who are attempting to control others are attempting to control others."

There are various types of manipulation, running from a pushy salesman to a sincerely oppressive accomplice—and a few practices are simpler to spot than others.

Here, specialists clarify several indications that could signify that one could be the subject of manipulation; you feel fear, commitment, and blame.

Manipulative conduct includes three variables:

- Fear, commitment, and blame.

"At the point when you are being controlled by somebody, you are as a rule mentally constrained into accomplishing something you most likely would prefer truly not to do. You may feel frightened to do it, commit to doing it, or blameworthy about not doing it.

The two regular manipulators are: "the domineering jerk" and "the person in question". A harasser causes you to feel fearful and might utilize hostility, dangers, and terrorizing to control you. The unfortunate casualty induces a sentiment of blame in their objective. "The injured individual, for the most part, acts hurt. Be that as it may, while manipulators frequently play the person in question, actually they are the ones who have caused the issue.

An individual who is focused by manipulators who play the injured individual, regularly attempt to help the manipulator so as to quit feeling remorseful. The manipulator often feels answerable for helping the injured individual by doing whatever they can to stop their torment.

- There are surprises

On the off chance that there are surprises, it means that manipulation is happening.

One kind of manipulator is 'Mr. Pleasant Guy.' This individual may be useful and do a ton of favors for others. It is confounding on the grounds that you don't understand that something negative is going on. Yet, then again, with each great deed, there is a string connected—a desire." If you don't meet the manipulator's desire, you will be described as selfish.

Truth be told, abusing the standards and desires for correspondence is one of the most widely recognized types of manipulation.

A salesman, for instance, may cause it to appear in the light of the fact that the person in question gave you an arrangement, you should purchase the item or in a relationship, an accomplice may get you to that point where they demand something consequently from you of which you must oblige to do. "These tactics work since they misuse social standards." It's entirely expected to respond favors.

However in any event, when somebody does one unscrupulously, we regularly still feel constrained to respond and consent."

You notice the 'foot-in-the-entryway' and 'entryway in-the-face' techniques.

Regularly, manipulators attempt one of two tactics. The first is the foot-in-the-entryway system, where somebody begins with a little and sensible solicitation—like, do you have the opportunity? — Which at that point leads into a bigger solicitation—like I need $10 for a taxi. "This is normally utilized in road tricks,"

The entryway in-the-face strategy is the inverse—it includes somebody making a major solicitation, having it dismissed, at that point making a little one...

Somebody doing contract work, for instance, may approach you for an enormous aggregate of cash in advance, and after you declined, will request a little sum, he says.

This works since, following the bigger solicitation, the smaller request appears to be more sensible,

Why Do People Manipulate?

People control you since they figure they won't get captured. Furthermore, in the event that they do get captured, they don't figure you'll do anything.

What makes them figure they won't get captured? If you portray cluelessness or gullibility. They see themselves understanding or knowing things that you don't.

If you have low comprehension of social elements, having issues with understanding jokes, are not quick to perceive a track until it's past the point of no return, can't recognize greatness from lewd gestures, can't tell when two people are teasing, at that point, people will control you, basically in light of the fact that they can. They realize you can't take care of something you don't realize they're doing. They see the shortcoming and exploit it.

What's more, for what reason do they figure you will do nothing? There are three reasons:

1. Because they can additionally utilize your cluelessness to state you're causing things to go up, or to attempt to divert you with side contentions;

2. Because they believe they can hurt you beyond what you can hurt them: truly, this is on the grounds that you're most likely excessively pleasant. They realize that on

account of a showdown, you won't have the option to take it far before separating;

3. Because in your negligence, you have not framed devotions to counter deceitfulness and anything that might occur. You, in contrast to your manipulators, have a social gathering for an organization, not for the support but to up in debates.

How to understand that? I don't believe being progressively particular or being less decent are good arrangements since they don't address the genuine reasons for the issue. The viable, long haul arrangement is to address every one of the three points of focus.

You have to improve your comprehension of human instinct and human inspirations. Start by observing that a great many people are not moved by ethics whether they think they'll be compensated when seen doing right and whether they think they'll be seen fouling up and rebuffed. That implies that in the event that you show shortcomings and offer the low likelihood of reprisal, it doesn't make a difference where you go, or who you're with, somebody will manhandle that.

You have to pick up the passionate equalization and detachment of desires with the goal that not many things can really hurt you. Never anticipate the best of people, since when you do, it makes you vulnerable to manipulation.

Become progressively mindful of social elements. Understand that a few people become a close acquaintance with one another for social assurance, not for adoration or for the organization.

I know numerous people right now who for obvious reasons, have endured the serious tactics of manipulation – which incorporates love-besieging, over the top obsessive lies, the horrendous consequence of triangulations and slanderous attacks, and practices which challenge any human explanation or clarification.

These things fly under the flag of 'manipulation.'

So, for what reason do a few people use manipulation as a strategy?

What in the world drives people to control as opposed to being bona fide?

I'd prefer to take you on an excursion for a more profound take a gander at 'manipulation.'

Manipulation Is About Fear and Unworthiness

What causes an individual to capitalize on utilizing the tactics of manipulation so as to attempt to verify an ideal motivation?

The main explanation is very self-explanatory – fear!

The fear that this individual won't increase an ideal outcome created from their own benefits, that life and others won't give well, that life and others are situated against this individual, that others would get what they want, and that there are restricted assets in a 'no-nonsense' world that must be verified and controlled so as to endure inwardly, basically, or monetarily, that what will my life be in the event that I don't get this going and will someone get the high ground over me on the event that I don't?

Presently how about we burrow further...

The fear beneath the demonstrations of manipulation, originates from an individual's absence of value.

This interprets as "I am not deserving of life working out for me", and "I am not deserving of life as others are having my eventual benefits on a basic level."

How an individual see that they identify with others and life, is basically how this individual sees themselves.

So, to improve, the genuine conviction is: I am dishonorable.

Manipulation Is About Lack Of Consciousness

The absence of cognizance happens when there is an inability to perceive that we are liable for our own world. Being oblivious is the failure to make the immediate relationship between one's life's occasions and inner degree of being.

What this relationship implies is this; it doesn't make a difference what anybody intentionally introduces to the world on the grounds that the passionate aim underneath that introduction is the genuine determinant of where their awareness lies and what will at last unfurl.

There is no beating the frameworks of so inside so without.

Oblivious people don't accept that this framework exists, notwithstanding the recurrent examples, the excruciating scenes, and the disgorging disillusionments. This is the embodiment of not gaining from past encounters, or what inward feelings and external life are appearing as.

This is the state of not advancing.

Oblivious people accept that manipulation in an apparent 'hazardous world' is the best approach to getting results, regardless of how these outcomes do not bring sturdy fulfillment and winding up genuinely or truly back at the starting point over and over.

At that point, to attempt to maintain a strategic distance from the agony of this – another manipulation should be made.

For what reason does manipulation payoff beyond the underlying 'handy solution'? Since the activity of manipulation isn't a successful or genuine activity, it is thus a guarded response as an attempt to balance fear, agony, and shame.

It is a purposeful activity that isn't adjusted in the cognizance of more prominent benefits.

A definitive degree of obviousness is the non-understanding. By attempting to make gain by means of manipulation, as opposed to genuineness, the individual outcome is non-valid.

Anything picked up from that degree of obviousness can and will just make empty triumphs, continuous agony, void, fear, and obviously more dishonor.

Dishonor is a desperate detachment from life and others – it is the fear of being disgraceful of not being adored and acknowledged by others and life as a whole.

It is a separation from oneness.

Along these lines, it is just people who feel disgraceful at the center of their control.

Stories about how to spot manipulators are extremely popular nowadays. A fast web search will turn up hundreds, if not a huge number of pages that depict narcissists and attempts to let you know precisely how to see the warning signs and act as the needs arises. These well-expected pieces attempt to tell you the best way to recognize a manipulator, name them, and maintain a strategic distance from them and also keeping in mind that, that is acceptable. I feel a profundity frequently with regards to when we attempt to paint the essence of evil spirits onto people with a wide brush without a consideration for subtlety, calmly tossing out findings here and names there, and we never appear to truly get down to the base of what's happening and really understanding the circumstance for what it is. This is what this book is attempting to solve, to increase a superior comprehension of the manipulator. Not the slightest bit does this book look to approve or support the activities of manipulative people, but to just give a stage for comprehension.

I was a manipulator for a large portion of the long stretches of my life, I'll let it known. I'll additionally say that I just didn't have the foggiest idea about any better. I was a truly terrible one as well, so let me disclose to you at the present time that this story originates from my direct understanding of what it resembled and what I'm similar to now. I needed to turn my own focal point internal and practice an extreme duty to change. This is somewhat me assuming liability for my own mix-ups, incompletely instructing them to you so you may better recognize the truth about and get manipulators, and ideally give some nice recommendations that will show you the proper behavior in like manner to limit strife and disarray.

A manipulative individual may state they need consideration when they're disturbed and simply need to be disregarded, at that point, appear to be totally tired of your quality — possibly pestered. They may forget about totally imperative pieces of a story with the expectation that you don't get it so they can cause you to appear the adversary, and unfortunately, they may convince you that you were off base. Have you encountered this or something like it? This is manipulation.

Communication

As we develop and experience an ever-increasing extent, we tend to adapt to commonly worthy methods of communicating with people. Had I been given the decision to either be or not be the manipulator I was before, I would have decided not to have gotten one, undoubtedly. I never had that decision. Manipulation, in my view, is a progression of educated practices and methods of speaking with the outside world, which are somewhat topsy-turvy. We take in our communication style from what functions admirably with others, and in the event that we figure out how to impart from useless people, we learn brokenness. Glancing back at my trades, I was continually confused, as regards the objectives of my manipulation with respect to why we were unable to appear to end up in agreement — this is regularly how manipulators put on a show of being so valid in their plans, in light of the fact that to them, it really is their source of existence. In the event that we can more readily comprehend what manipulative people are really attempting to let us know, in the appearing coded language they've learned, we can likely figure out how to speak with them and diffuse circumstances.

If we can get familiar with the strategies used to impart things which are unique in relation to what they're letting us know, we can in any event to some degree unravel what they're really attempting to state to us — and we can react likewise, as opposed to surrendering everything over to risk, uncovering our helpless selves to the manipulator's control.

Indeed Means Maybe

For some, manipulative people, they've basically figured out how to request things the incorrect way. "Truly", might mean no and "yes" might mean perhaps, which is a startling idea in our current reality where assent is vital for a ton of social connections — I've thought that it was ideal to request that people affirm their point of view a few times before arriving at decisions about where they stand. I have discovered that it's ideal to give people a few possibilities, in a happy tone, to change their feelings and express their genuine thoughts straightforwardly. Numerous people have figured out how to say "no", once in a while when they truly need something from excessively severe guardians, at times from oppressive guardians. Not being manipulative isn't the deficiency of manipulative people, it is their obligation.

The truth of the matter is, with manipulative people, "yes" consistently signifies "perhaps" and is liable to change anytime.

The Child Within

At last, most manipulators are youngsters. They are not totally dependable and I think what a great many people botch as a purposeful demonstration, a well-considered, plotted, conspired up-approach to screw them over, is simply the manipulator. This isn't to overlook it — striking duplicity is rarely right. This is to state that on the off chance that we need to comprehend and figure out how to adequately manage manipulative people, we have to address the youngster inside, not to the outward veil they present to us.

This was me. I was intense, savage, valiant, and free. Inside, I was apprehensive and startled. In the event that an issue occurred in an individual circumstance, I would close it down, truly finding a workable pace out of an open café leaving the individual who I'd felt had wronged me to pay. That wasn't right, and fortunately, I've been compensated for those occasions now. It's just plain obvious, the main explanation I could be solid was by removing immense lumps of reality to make my internal world totally sheltered, and numerous manipulators do likewise. I required a presentation to this present reality piece by piece, and numerous stunning people helped me through this procedure.

CHAPTER 6:

How To Understand If People Want To Manipulate Us And Recognize Persuasion Techniques

Persuasion is an interesting topic. There are lots of persuasions that are considered just fine in society. They are acceptable, and even some people hold jobs where they will spend a lot of time trying to persuade others. Any attempt by one person to influence someone else to do some action can be persuasion. A salesperson at a car dealership is using persuasion because they try to persuade someone to purchase a new vehicle. This isn't seen as something sinister or bad. The difference here is that this persuasion and other similar examples of persuasion benefit both parties. The car dealer makes a sale and some money, and the "victim" is going to get a new vehicle.

There are lots of legitimate types of persuasion that aren't considered part of dark psychology. The car dealer story above is a typical example. If a negotiator uses their skills to persuade a terrorist to let their hostage go, this is a good form of persuasion. If you convince someone to come along to an event that they will enjoy, then this is a good form of persuasion. This type of persuasion is seen as positive persuasion. But then, what would count as dark persuasion?

Understanding Dark Persuasion

The first difference you will notice between positive and dark persuasion is the motive behind it. Positive persuasion is used in order to encourage someone to complete an action that isn't going to cause them any harm. In some cases, such as with the negotiator saving a hostage, this persuasion can be used to help save lives.

But with dark persuasion, there isn't really any form of a moral motive. The motive is usually amoral and often immoral. If positive persuasion is understood as a way to help people help themselves, then dark persuasion is more of the process of making people act against their own self-interest. Sometimes, people are going to do these actions begrudgingly, knowing that they are probably not making the right choice, but they do it because they are eager to stop the incessant persuasion efforts. In other cases, the best dark persuader is going to make their victim think that they acted wisely, but the victim is actually doing the opposite in that case. So, what are the motivations for someone who is a dark persuader? This is going to depend on the situation and the individual who is doing the persuading. Some people like to persuade their victims in order to serve their own self-interests. Others are going to act through with the intention just to cause some harm to the other person. In some cases, the persuader is not going to really benefit from darkly persuading their victim, but they do so because they want to inflict pain on the other person. And still, others enjoy the control that this kind of persuasion gives to them. You will also find that the outcome you get from dark persuasion is going to differ from what happens with positive persuasion. With positive persuasion, you are going to get one of three scenarios, including the following:

- The benefit goes to the person who is being persuaded.

- There is a win/win benefit for the persuaded and the persuader.

- There is a mutual benefit for the person who is persuaded and a third party.

All of these outcomes are good because they will involve a positive result for the person who is being persuaded.

Sometimes, there will be others who benefit from these actions. But out of all three situations, the persuaded party is always going to benefit.

With dark persuasion, the outcome is going to be very different. The persuader is the one who will always benefit when they exercise their need for influence or control. The one who is being persuaded often goes against what is in their self-interest when they listen, and they are not going to benefit from all this dark persuasion.

In addition, the most skilled dark persuaders are not only able to cause some harm to their victims while also benefiting themselves, but they could also end up harming others in the process.

Unmasking the Dark Persuader

At this point, you may be curious about who is using these dark methods of persuasion. Are there actually people out there who are interested in using this kind of persuasion and using it against others to cause harm?

The main characteristics of a dark persuader are either indifference toward or an inability to care about how persuasion is going to impact others. Such people who use this kind of persuasion are going to often be narcissistic and will see their own needs as more important than the needs of others.

They may even be sociopathic and unable to grasp the idea of someone else's emotions.

Many times this kind of dark persuasion is going to show up in a relationship. Often one but sometimes both partners are going to be inclined towards trying to use dark persuasion on each other.

If these attempts are persistent and endure, then this type of relationship is going to be classified as psychologically abusive, and that is not healthy for the victim.

Often times, they will not realize that there is something going on or that they are darkly persuaded until it is too late and they are stuck there.

There are many examples of using this kind of dark persuasion in a relationship.

If one partner stops the other partner from taking a new job opportunity or doesn't allow them to go out with friends, then this could be an example of dark persuasion.

The dark persuader will work to convince the victim that they are acting in a way that is best for the relationship. In reality, the victim is going through a process that harms them and the relationship.

Dark Persuasion Techniques to Be on the Lookout For

After taking a look at the different types of persuasion and what they all mean, you may be able to see why dark persuasion is such a bad thing and can be harmful to the victim. Being able to recognize the different techniques that the manipulator may use can make it easier to understand when it is being used on you.

So, how exactly is a dark persuader able to use this idea in order to carry out their wishes? There are a few different tactics that a dark manipulator uses, but some of the most common options include:

The Long Con

The first method that we are going to look at is the Long Con. This method is kind of slow and drawn out, but it can be really effective because it takes so long and is hard to recognize or even pinpoint when something went wrong. Some of the main reasons some people may have the ability to resist persuasions are because they feel that they are being pressured by the other person, and this can make them back off. If they feel that there is a lack of rapport or trust with the person who is trying to persuade them, they will steer clear as well. The Long Con is so effective because they are able to overcome these main problems and give the persuader exactly what they want.

The Long Con allows the dark persuader to take their time to work in order to earn the trust of their victim. They will to take some time to befriend the victim and make sure that their victim trusts and likes them. This is going to be achieved by the persuader with artificial rapport building, which sometimes seems excessive, and other techniques that will help to increase the comfort levels between the persuader and their victim.

As soon as the persuader sees that the victim is properly readied psychologically, the persuader is going to begin their attempts. They may start out with some insincere positive persuasion. The persuader is going to lead their victim into making a choice or doing some actions that will actually benefit the persuader. This is going to serve the persuader in two ways. First, the victim starts to become used to persuasion by that persuader, the second is that the victim is going to start making that mental association between a positive outcome and the persuasion.

The Long Con takes a long period of time to complete because the persuader doesn't want to make it too obvious what they are doing. An example of this is that of a recently widowed lady who is vulnerable because of her age and from her bereavement. After her loss, a man starts to befriend her. This man may be someone she knows from church or even a relative. He starts to spend more time with her, showing immense kindness and patience, and it doesn't take too long for her guard to drop when he comes around.

Then this man starts to carry out some smaller acts of positive persuasions that we mentioned earlier. He may advise her of what bank account to use or a better way to reduce any monthly bills. The victim is going to appreciate these efforts and the fact that the man is trying to help her, and she takes the advice.

After some time, the man then tries to use some dark persuasion. He may try to persuade her to let him invest some of her money. She obliges because of the positive persuasion that was used in the past. Of course, the man is going to work to take everything he can get from her. If the manipulator is skilled enough, she may feel that he actually tried to help her, but the money is lost because he just ran into some bad luck with the investment. This is how far dark persuasion can go.

Gradualism

Most times when we hear about acts of dark persuasion, it seems impossible and unbelievable. What we fail to realize is that this dark persuasion isn't ever going to be a big or a sudden request that comes out of nowhere. Dark persuasion is more like a staircase, the dark persuader is never going to ask the victim to do something big and dramatic the first time they meet, instead, they will have the victim take one step at a time.

When the manipulator has the target only go one step at a time, the whole process seems like less of a big deal. Before the victim knows it, they have already gone a long way down, and the persuader isn't likely to let them leave or come back up again.

Let's take an example of how this process is going to look in real life. Let's say that there is a criminal who wanted to make it so that someone else committed the crimes for them. Gang bosses, cult leaders, and even Charles Manson did this exact same thing.

This criminal wouldn't dream of beginning the process by asking their victim to murder for them. This would send out a red flag, and no one in their right minds would willingly go out and kill for someone they barely know. Instead, the criminal would start out by having the victim do something small like a petty crime or simply hiding a weapon for them. Something that isn't that big of a deal for the victim, at least in comparison.

Over time, the acts that the manipulator is able to persuade their victim to do will become more severe. And since they did the smaller crimes, the persuader now has the unseen leverage of holding some of those smaller misdeeds over the victim, kind of like for blackmail. Before the victim knows it, they are going to feel like they are in too deep. They will then be persuaded to carry out some of the most shocking crimes. And often, by this point, they will do it because they feel like they have no other choice.

Dark persuaders are going to be experts at using this gradualism to help increase the severity of their persuasion over time. They know that no victim would be willing to jump the canyon or do the big crime or misdeed right away. So, the persuader works to build a bridge to get there. By the time the victim sees how far in they are, it is too late to turn back.

Masking the True Intentions

There are different methods that a persuader is able to use dark psychology in order to get the things that they want. Disguising their true desires is very important for them to be successful. The best persuaders can use this approach in a variety of ways, but the method they choose is often going to depend on the victim and the situation.

One principle that is used by a persuader is the idea that many people are going to have a difficult time refusing two requests when they happen in a row. Let's say that the persuader wants to get $200 from the victim, but they do not intend to repay the money. To start, the persuader may begin by saying that they need a loan for the amount of $1000. They may go into some details about the consequences to themselves if the persuader doesn't come up with that kind of money sometime soon.

It may happen that the victim feels some kind of guilt or compassion to the persuader, and they want to help, but $1000 is a lot of money, more than the victim is able to lend. From here, the persuader is going to lessen their request from $1000 down to $200, the amount that they wanted from the beginning. Of course, there is some kind of emotional reason for needing the money, and the victim feels like it is impossible to refuse this second request. They want to help out the persuader, and they feel bad for not giving in to the initial request when they were asked. In the end, the persuader gets the $200 they originally wanted, and the victim is not going to know what has taken place.

Another type of technique that the persuader can use is known as reverse psychology. This can also help to mask true intentions during the persuasion. Some people have a personality that is known as a boomerang. This means that they will refuse to go in the direction that they are thrown and instead will veer off into different directions.

If the persuader knows someone who is more of a boomerang type, then they are able to identify a key weakness of that person. For example, let's say that a persuader has a friend who is attempting to win over some girl they like. The persuader knows that the friend will use and then hurt that girl. The girl is currently torn between a malicious friend and an innocent third party. The persuader may try to steer the girl in the direction of the guy who is actually a good choice, knowing that she is going to go against this and end up going with the harmful friend.

Leading Questions

Another method of dark persuasion that can be used is known as leading questions. If you have ever had an encounter with a salesman that is skilled, verbal persuasion can be really impactful when it is deployed in careful and calibrated ways. One of the most powerful techniques that can be used verbally is leading questions.

These leading questions are going to be any questions that are intended to trigger a specific response out of the victim. The persuader may ask the target something like "how bad do you think those people are?" This question is going to imply that the people the persuader is asking about are definitely bad to some extent. They could have chosen to ask a question that was no leading such as "how do you feel about those people?"

Dark persuaders are masters at using leading questions in a way that is hard to catch. If the victim ever begins to feel that they are being led, then they are going to resist, and it is hard to lead them or persuade them.

If a persuader ever senses that their victim starts to catch what is happening, they will quit using that one and switch over to another one. They may come back to that tactic, but only when the victim has quieted down a bit and is more likely to be influenced again.

The Law of State Transference

The state is a concept that takes a look at the general mood someone is in. If someone is aligned with their deeds, words, and thoughts, then this is an example of a strong and congruent state. The law of state transference involves the concept of someone who holds the balance of power in a situation and can then transfer their emotional state onto the other person they are interacting with. This can be a very powerful tool for the dark persuader to use against their victim.

Initially, the influencer is going to force their own state to match the state that their target naturally has. If the target is sad and they talk slowly, the influencer is going to make their own state follow this format. The aim is to create a deep rapport with the target.

After we get to this state match, the influencer is then going to alter their own state subtly and see if they have some compliance for the victim. Perhaps, they will choose to speed up their own voice to see if the victim will speed up as well. Once the victim starts to show these signs of compliance, then this is an indication that the influencer is at the hook point.

As soon as this hook point is reached, though it may take some time depending on the target and the situation, then the influencer would change their own personal state to the one they want the victim to have. This could be an emotional state that the influencer wants. It could be positive, angry, happy, or indignant. It often depends on what the persuader wants to help reach their goals. This technique is an important one for a dark persuader because it is going to show the impact of subconscious cues on the failure or the success of any type of persuasion.

CHAPTER 7:

How To Understand And Manage Emotions And Those Of Others

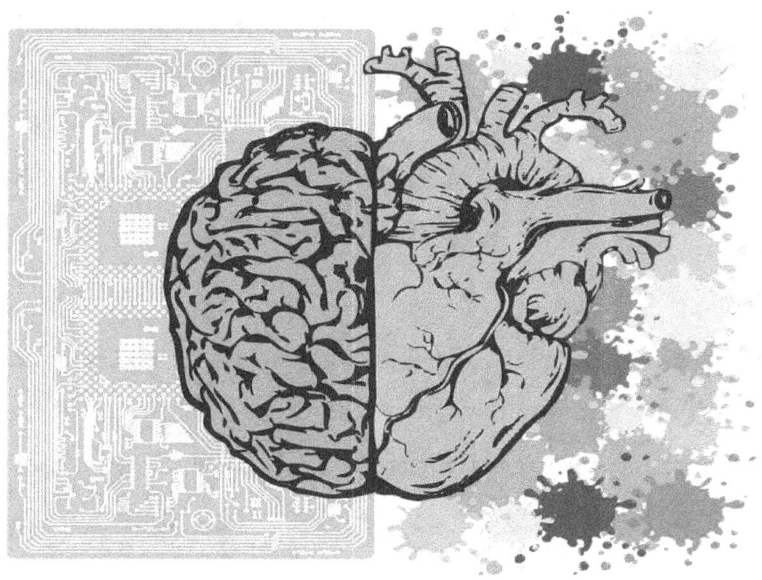

Understanding Your Emotions

A huge part of having a high level of emotional intelligence is, understanding your own emotions. It's easy to pick out certain things that we feel, but to know what they're trying to tell us about ourselves is even more challenging to understand. Throughout this chapter, we will give you all the essential steps needed for you to really get what's going on inside of your head. It involves effective communication, creating the right emotional environment, and managing the thoughts and feelings that you have. We'll also discuss the disadvantages as well as the benefits that your emotional state provides you.

This is something that will need to be continually practiced. We are merely giving you the first essential steps to get started along your journey of self-reflection. Emotional intelligence differs from any other practice you have because it requires constant growth. Growing your EQ isn't an overnight process, nor is there any limit to how emotionally intelligent and self-aware you can be.

Remember, throughout this process, that awareness isn't always just criticism or encouragement. There is a crucial spectrum that we have to understand the difference between understanding the good and evil in all situations and all individuals.

Don't be afraid to admit the truth to yourself, and when you do come face to face with an issue that might be more challenging to handle, it's OK to take a break! While the journey of emotional intelligence will never end, it's OK to take a break and just rest along the side of the road for a while.

Effective Communication

Communication is one of the most critical parts of your job as an effective leader. It is the center of every interaction that you will have with your employees. Communication affects the way that they see you, and the way that you see them. Communication is essential for sharing emotions, as well as coming up with proactive solutions to get the job done.

What Is Communication?

A lot of the time, we think it is just the words that we say to each other. There's a lot more to communication that we need to understand. It is your tone of voice, how you say it, how you use your body, it is when you choose to say it and why you wish to bring certain things up, and so on. Communication also involves things that we don't share with other people. Sometimes you might feel the need to keep certain information from those who would otherwise wish to know it. This will be something that you have to consider, as well. Just because the truth is out there, does not mean that you should tell everybody. Is there a different way to say to them? Sometimes you might be crossing specific moral barriers. The better that you understand all of these aspects, the easier it will be for you to find the right solution. Before we talk about practical communication skills, let's just take a look at a few other things that can cause unhealthy communication. The first thing is, not fully listening to another person. Way too often, we sit there and think about what we're going to say rather than listening to them. This can cause the other person to feel frustrated, and then it just makes the whole situation ugly.

If you aren't effectively listening, that means that you don't understand what the point of the conversation is, in the first place. We also have to make sure that we hold our judgment from the other person that's sharing with us. It is effortless to come up with a quick understanding around what somebody else is discussing, but if we show this, it can make them scared, and they no longer want to share as much with us. Communication should feel open and accepting, and if somebody else feels like they don't have this environment, then they won't be completely open and honest in their communication. We need everyone to be as transparent as possible.

With that being said, let's look at a few things that will help you create a positive communicative environment. The first one is, always open and willing to listen. Let those that you lead know that they can come to you at any time they need to. While it is easy to say this, you also have to make sure that you show how much you actually care and are willing to listen.

Actions will always speak louder than words, no matter what anyone else tells you. Hold your judgment, have a neutral but welcoming facial expression, and a calm tone when people are describing things to you. Use smiles and keep your body open.

Don't cross your arms because it can make you look a little bit more closed off. Avoid sitting with your hands on your hips because it can seem too authoritative. Instead, sit down and stay on the same level as the other person. If you are standing over them while they're sitting or they're standing over you while you are sitting, it can create an imbalance of power, and it could alter the way that you both communicate with each other.

Make sure that you are also very clear, as well. Too often, there'll be some leaders who are very cryptic about what they are trying to say. Not everyone will pick up on little messages so, if you have something to say, just say it. Even if it might be a bit harsh, sometimes you can still have a calmer tone and a more open demeanor to make it come off.

Empathy will be your best friend in this whole situation, that's why having emotional intelligence, is so important. If somebody comes to you with a problem, and maybe they had messed up and made a big mistake, you still need to show empathy. It can be tough to do this, but as you practice increasing your EQ levels, you'll discover that it is a lot easier to show empathy to other people. They need to be able to trust you, and there should be an open environment where everybody can express themselves as they need.

When it comes to listening, make sure that you are also doing your best to show them that you have open ears. Don't just come back with comments after they tell you something. Ask questions to get more information. Other people will feel more open when they can take the lead and start to talk about themselves, so asking questions allows them to do this.

When you feel angry and reactive, don't react right away. Take some time to think about it. You can use a question like, "Do you really feel this way?" Or, "Is there anything else you think I should know about what's important?" because this will encourage them to continue opening up and sharing what's truly going on. They'll reveal more information, and you can have a minute to process the things that they're saying. Whatever you do, make sure that you maintain a reasonable level of eye contact and don't be distracted with other things. As a leader, you are probably going to be busy all the time getting texts, emails, phone calls, and so on. Put your phone down and face away from the computer when you are talking to them. While it might seem like you don't have the time to do this, it will be better for you in the long run. It will be a lot quicker than you think.

Let's take a look at some other essential tips that will help make sure that you have a healthy emotional environment.

This way, it will be a lot easier for you to have communication in the end as well. It is a practice that will come naturally to you after you improve your necessary skills.

Emotional Climate

Many things will affect the overall emotional climate of your workspace. It will be determined by the different state of feelings both you and your employees feel. This can vary from floor to floor or team to team. Let's think of a hospital, for example. Hospitals have different departments and many of them are on different levels. Let's imagine that the intensive care unit is on the sixth floor, and the maternity ward is on the eighth floor. If you were to step off on the sixth floor, as soon as you get off the elevator, you'd probably feel some form of intensity. The intensive care unit is where critical patients go, and not everybody makes it out okay. There are many grieving families and general worry over the fate of these patients. If you went up to the maternity ward on the eighth floor where babies are being born, the ambiance would be one of encouragement, happiness, and of course, relative relaxation. While there might still be a couple of people who are struggling because they might have children who are in more severe conditions, there will always be plenty of happy families that are celebrating and excited about life.

This is just one example of how the emotional climate can change, even when most of the settings are the same. The first thing you'll want to do in building the right emotional environment is to identify what it is like now. There are usually one or two things that are pretty obvious about the worst part of the job. If you are in a customer service call center, the worst part is probably dealing with some of the more challenging customers. If you are in a news station, sometimes the most significant stressor is the urgency to launch and publish essential articles.

Whatever the most significant stressor might be in your work environment, tune into this, because it will reveal a lot about what you need to do to increase the overall emotional mood. After you've identified this, do some self-reflecting and see if you can come up with what your most significant weaknesses might be in the emotional climate of everybody else. The first thing that we have to remember is that we teach other people how they should be treating us. If you are mean and scary to every employee that you have, they're going to treat you like you are a creepy monster. They're going to be afraid of you, and they won't want to share the truth with you. When you come around, they're going to hide. Not literally, but in their emotional state, they will make sure to stay cold and closed off because they're terrified of what you might do to them.

At the same time, if you treat everybody like nothing matters, and it is all just a big fun party, then they're going to think that you are the life of the party, instead of a leader. You have to find the right balance between them. You'll want to show some restrictions and a little bit of a strict personality, but at the same time, it should never be something cold that cuts people off. Empathy will come in quite handy here. Have meetings where you can discuss not just work performance, but work moods. We can give you tips on how to build your empathy, but at the same time, it is a considerable practice. You have to get to know your employees on an individual level. You'll have to hear from them. You need to give them the chance to say their side of the story to tell you what they might not like and give you practical advice about how you can make a better environment for them. You also have to remember that you need to create an emotional environment built on bonds. This isn't just the connections between you and your employees. Your employees should be friends with each other as well. When you can create a big family, it makes things better for everyone involved. In a group of friends, sometimes people get along, but not everybody looks out for one another's best interests. Think of it as a family. Not everybody is perfect, but at the end of the day, we can come together and make sure that we look out for ourselves and the members of our family. If you can create this kind of close environment, then people will not only perform well so that they do good, but they'll perform well because they want the rest of their team to do great

Emotional Management

A considerable part of creating a positive and productive emotional climate is making sure that you are managing your own emotions. It is not easy to get to know ourselves. There are times where we might not fully understand what our emotions are. Perhaps you are somebody who already has a high level of emotional intelligence, and you are just looking to help other people. You could also be somebody who has never heard of emotional intelligence before and now you are trying to figure out what you can do to increase yours. Whether you are a beginner or you are a little bit more experienced, we're going to have similar interactions that will help make sure that you perform the best way possible. The first thing that we all need to do is just to take some time. This can be really hard anytime you feel anger, resentment, rage, frustration, confusion, and anything else that may be challenging to deal with. However, you will have to learn how to just to take a minute and step back. If you try and figure out how to work out your emotions as you are experiencing it, then it can make things less difficult.

Make sure that you avoid using labels all the time as well. Just because you feel angry doesn't mean that you have to react in a way that is common to when somebody is experiencing that feeling. Again, stress and anxiety puts pressure on your mind to respond right away. Perhaps you have the desire to make a new policy immediately because you are desperate for better results. This can just create more problems if we don't have time to think of our reaction correctly. We have to really sit down and look at things all the way through before we create new rules and regulations. When we don't, it means that we'll just end up making things harder for ourselves and the end.

Deal with each new situation as if it were its own instead of resorting to past methods of resolution. It can be hard not to compare it to the past, but we can't use everything we've been through as a clear definitive way to judge what we're passing through now. You should learn from your mistakes, and it is important to look through the things that we've already done, to see what can be taken away from us. At the same time, we can't judge the outcome as being the same. Think about what worked in the past and what did it, that's as far as it needs to go. Don't attach a current situation to the same emotional state that you were the first time this had happened.

What matters most throughout your emotional management process is that your self-awareness helps give you direct insight into the emotions that you are feeling and why you might be feeling that way. Don't give yourself the chance to be anxious and to start freaking out about what might happen. Stay calm, relaxed, and collected, and look inwards before you ever blame somebody else for your emotion. See the ways you affected it yourself on an individual level. While there are certainly people who can influence our state of feelings, nobody else is responsible for our emotions.

You control what you feel. This is probably the only thing that you have control over, even if you are in a position of leadership.

That doesn't mean that you are the boss of everybody all the time. You simply set the rules for the workplace. Our most significant power is our own emotional state. As soon as we blame other people for our emotions, we give that power away, which means that we are left entirely helpless.

If somebody came up to you and started poking you, calling you names, pushing you around, and in general, being mean, of course, they have more of a role in your emotional state than somebody else who's just sitting in the back out of the spotlight.

Still, you are the one in charge of how you choose to feel after this. It will be really hard, and you will more likely feel bad about yourself when somebody is actively trying to make you feel that way. It'll be harder to manage, but it is still something that is directly under our control.

The Disadvantages of Your Emotions

Having a high level of emotional intelligence means that you are self-aware, and you'll be able to reflect a healthy and positive way that creates an excellent work environment. At the same time, we have to be highly aware of all the disadvantages that our emotional state can have. When you aren't properly managing your emotions, a lot of bad things can happen. Let's take a look at what a few of those are.

First and foremost, what you'll do is create a false perspective. Simply put, sympathy is something that many of us have, and it is beneficial in some circumstances. Empathy, however, is a greater understanding of somebody else's emotional state, and it gives you a clear perspective on what is going on.

For example, let's say that somebody asks you if they could borrow some money. Sympathy is feeling bad for them and giving them the money because you don't want them to be sad anymore. Empathy is when you've experienced poverty yourself, and you might have gone through financial hardships that make it easier for you to understand how awful it feels to have to ask somebody for money. You are giving them the money, not because you feel bad for them and it makes you sad, and you don't want to feel bad anymore. You are giving them the money because you are empathetic. You know what it feels like to go through that situation, and you're more focused on taking the pain away from them, not considering how it might alleviate your own emotions.

You don't want anybody to have to experience that negative situation. That's what empathy is. This will give you the right perspective. You can see things not only from your point of view but from theirs as well. When we're sympathetic, we only see things through our eyes, and we see them in a way where the other person experiences something negative and we can provide them with a positive outcome. Empathy is doing something that works well for everyone.

When you are emotionally managing yourself, this can mean that you end up using your feelings to guide you through everything. You are going to act impulsively, and you are only going to make decisions based on the things that you are experiencing. You might have frustration, anger, or even moments of high excitement.

If you are not really considering what these emotions mean and looking deep within yourself, then it starts to make you feel a little bit more impulsive. You are going to act on instinct and do the first thing that comes to mind.

We have to consider how this affects our positive emotions, as well. Of course, if you are angry and frustrated, it can make you act out right away. At the same time, when you are too excited, you are enthusiastic and ready for something great to happen, and you aren't really looking at the practical way to get there. In some cases, this could be even worse because you become so excited that you are blind to anything wrong that could happen. Then something terrible does happen, and you feel even worse afterward, creating more feelings of frustration, anger, and resentment.

Just because you have a positive emotion and a good feeling doesn't mean that you should act impulsively on that either. You can still be excited about things, but just make sure you consider all the good and all the bad of every situation.

The Benefits of Your Emotions

There's often a stereotype of that boss who is clueless while all their employees get together and talk about their many flaws. The reason that emotional intelligence can be so beneficial is that there is a level of social awareness in addition to the self-awareness that you will be practicing on your own. The social awareness means that you can understand the perception that other people have a view. This is just one of the many benefits of your emotions.

If you learn how to navigate your emotions right, they can be like the instruction manual for how you feel and what you need to do in your life to get the things that you want. Understanding your emotions means understanding your passions and fears. When you start to get angry about something, you might find that helps you realize what's most important to you. For example, think about the last time a parent was mad at their child.

They likely weren't mad at them just because that's how they felt at that moment; they were probably angry at them because they were afraid of their child's future. Maybe they became anxious thinking that the child was making the wrong decision. Of course, this isn't always the case, but many people will be angry when they feel as though something is taken away from them. At the same time, being angry can help show that you are passionate about them.

What is it that you care about? What are you afraid of never accomplishing and your future? When you start developing a better understanding of the things that you care about the most, it will make it easier to know how actually to achieve these things. Not only will your emotions give you greater insight into yourself, but they will also help you understand those around you. Many individuals can act a little irrationally. They might show fear and anxiety, and they can just generally do other things that might make it hard to understand them. When you can understand what emotion really is at the core, then you'll know better what other people might be trying to get from their life. This is important when it comes to being a leader to other people. Sometimes other people aren't even aware of what their emotions mean or what they might be trying to tell them. When you understand this, then you cannot help them out. We don't know how other people feel all the time, and we especially can't tell them how they think. Not everybody wants to hear that they're angry or that they're sad or that they're acting irrationally. However, you can still take this vital information and try to come up with a beneficial solution that will help you all in the end.

Response Versus Reaction

We have to understand the difference between a reaction and our response. Our reaction is an emotional feeling that you have as a result of a different situation. The answer is the action that you choose to take because of this feeling. Let's think of a common example. There are a group of friends playing a game together. One of them loses the game, they get agitated, they walk over to a different room, and they punch a wall. Can you identify what the reaction and response to the situation is? The result is anger. It is okay to be angry. While it is just a game at the end of the day, some individuals are just more passionate about these kinds of things. Sometimes we're in control of the level of anger that we feel and other times it is just an emotion that happens. The response is punching the wall. This is not okay when you take aggression out on yourself and other things around you. That will have a negative result for you and the people involved in this situation.

It is not wrong for that person to feel angry, but it is wrong for them to take it out on somebody else. This is the same for how we respond in a fight.

If somebody is screaming at you, telling you that you are worthless or that you do no good, and that you have no value, then you might get upset and angry with them and punch them.

First of all, let's acknowledge that what they're doing is not right.

It is never okay to make somebody feel bad like that.

Secondly, the anger you feel is valid, you have every right to feel this way. Even though you are in control of your emotions, we can't always help every little thing that we think, is wrong like in punching the other person.

The right way to respond would be to handle your emotions and talk it out with them in a productive way. Instead, it can turn into a fight, where each person is trying to outdo the other and have the last word. That doesn't help anyone and only creates more stress and anxiety in the individual.

Ensure you understand the differences between how you feel and how you take that feeling out in the world around you. Again, think of a workplace setting. You process a sales report, and you see that your team has been down by 10% since the last quarter. This is unacceptable because you are hoping to increase by 30%.

You get upset and frustrated and angry with them, thinking that it was all entirely their fault for not having a productive quarter. You hold a team meeting, and you share these ideas with them and in response, you decide to take away the holiday party coming up.

Everybody gets upset and angry, and one person even quits.

While it is perfectly acceptable and reasonable for you to be upset about these results, acting emotionally and irrationally isn't going to help the overall situation. Everyone is just going to be afraid of you now. Rather than being encouraged to continue moving forward, they will be angry and resentful toward you. It is vital that you understand what the reaction was in this situation. The response was stress and anxiety, which was excellent. Anyhow you feel when looking at that sales report is totally within your control, as is how you choose to feel. Your feelings and emotions are valid. It is the reaction that people can get upset about a proper response. Wait, it is patient and understanding and you have a healthy perspective if we can see both sides of the story.

It won't always be a clear cut, black and white road to understanding the difference between your response and your reaction, but it is something that we need to start practicing.

Emotional Manipulation

Emotional manipulation can happen at various levels. We have already known that fear is a very powerful emotion but that's not the only one. How about greed? That works just a good as fear. People who are driven by ambition can be easily caught with statements such as "think of all the money you could make." Such a statement would drive a greedy person over the edge. By the same token, if you're dealing with someone who is overly frugal, a statement such as "think of all the money you could save" would hit their sweet spot. The point here is that you need to know the person you're dealing with in order to make your manipulation attempts ring true. So, let's take a look at some emotional manipulation tactics which you can use in a given situation.

The Bait and Switch

This technique is predicated on a person pretending to be someone they are not until they get what they want. For example, a person who is interested in gaining something from another may pretend to be romantically interested in this person.

The victim, who is desperate for love and affection, will go along with the hopes of entering a meaningful relationship.

The manipulator then gets close enough to their target until they extract the benefit they seek. Once the manipulator gets what they want, they pull the bait and switch; that is, they revert to their true self. This type of technique is used to prey on the emotional needs of a person and is not limited to romantic relationships.

This can also occur when a manipulator senses that someone is desperate to make money. The manipulator then uses this need to manipulate the victim with the promise of easy money or a steady income. The victim goes along only to be defrauded at some point.

In a manner of speaking, the manipulation takes place every time the manipulator is able to strike a chord with the victim. The victim falls prey for the empty promises of the manipulator until either the manipulator reveals their true self, or just moves on.

The Blame Game

This is very common in the workplace. There are folks who are experts at pinning everything on someone else. For instance, when something goes wrong, the manipulator will find a way to shift the blame to someone else. The ablest manipulators are able to produce compelling evidence against others thereby clearing their name of any responsibility. Then, there are folks who are just full of excuses for the shortcomings. These folks tend to wear out their welcome quickly and need to move on sooner rather than later. The blame game can happen in relationships, business dealings, and politics. Politicians who find someone else to blame for the problems happening in their country often present themselves as saviors and heroes for their people. They are the ones who have a solution for everything, yet when you drill down on their track record, they really don't achieve much of anything.

Guilt

Guilt is one of the most powerful manipulation techniques known to humankind. Guilt can be used to manipulate people by making them feel inferior for the help and support they have received at some point. Guilt can also be used to get others to feel inadequate for a condition they possess. Think of all those times you hear people say, "Things would be different if you weren't sick." That is one of the most rudimentary means of making someone feel guilty, yet it is highly powerful. Also, you may hear others say things like, "remember when you needed my help? Now, I need your help." This is a clear attempt at coaxing someone to go along with the manipulator's intentions.

The White Knight

This game is used by skilled manipulators. In this game, the manipulator purposely creates a problem and then rushes to the rescue. The intention is to create dependency among those around them as the manipulator is the only one who can solve the problems they encounter. However, the victims may not be aware that the problems are artificially fabricated by the "white knight" to make them look good.

This is an expression of the problem-reaction-solution technique. In this technique, manipulators create a problem or exacerbate an existing one, then get people to react in a certain manner so that they can come to the rescue with the miracle solution.

So, the next time you ask yourself where certain people get these miraculous solutions in desperate times; don't be surprised if you happen to find yourself in the midst of a master manipulator.

CHAPTER 8:

What To Do And How To Behave If People Want To Manipulate Us

In this section, you will learn how people try to manipulate you and then learn some basic tools that you can use to handle that form of manipulation. Now there are much more advanced techniques, but we'll talk about the simple one. Now, let us talk about what the difference between manipulation and cohesion is. Cohesion involves the explicit use of force or threat, which means somebody, is threatening you, but that is not what you're talking about here. We are talking about manipulation, which tends to be devious and indirect, and it is not in your best interest.

You are not in the best interest of the target, whereby there are threats and the threats are subdued or implied as opposed to direct.

Cohesion is more like somebody putting a gun to your head while manipulation means putting a gun to their head to make it to do something or implying something bad about you. Deception is something that you can't have in manipulation.

A person that is doing the manipulation actually believes what they are saying. So, they are not lying.

That is why sometimes it is very hard to spot them because they actually believe what they are saying, and they don't deny the event, but they denied the meaning of the event, however, sometimes the false belief can almost be delusional.

Now, what is the ultimate solution? We have talked about the types of people, and we have talked about the specific type of toxicity, so now what is the solution for dealing with this problem.

It is very simple to deal with this problem, and the best way to deal with it is to cut these people from your life. It is very simple, but most times, people forget that it is an option.

How To Apply These Techniques Against A Manipulator

Let's look at some of the ways of how you might apply this technique. Now let's assume that you have a client putting her head on the left and screaming and saying that you didn't say or do something that she wanted you to do. So how do you respond to this kind of situation? The first one is to start begging her. But begging her is wrong because you are becoming overly helpful and you're obviously emotionally engaged.

The next one is to call the police to drag her to a psychic hospital. Now, this is a problem too because you are overly punishing her, and she may make up something and complain to the medical board about abusing your powers or something like that. Or she may want to sue you because she was injured by the police.

So, this is an overreaction in the other way, and of course, you don't want to be directly involved by wrestling with her. So, all these are the kinds of reasons that she can sue you or report you against, and also you don't want to be so disconnected whereby you are completely indifferent to what she's doing.

And you just walk down the hall, get a cup of coffee and check your email and just basically ignore her because that will even bring more intense responses.

So, an appropriate response is to wait for her and acknowledge her distress and then continue with the interaction. So, you learn to be a non-reactive listener.

Know What You Want And How You Feel

The first one is to know what you want and how you feel. When you are connected to yourself, and you really love yourself, you will know if helping somebody or giving something to somebody is going to be good for you. If you are ready to give something to somebody else, you would check if it's coming from inside of you and coming from a genuine loving place and not from a place of guilt, shame, or manipulation. You will know if it is coming from you, and if you genuinely want to do that thing because you don't want to feel guilty about it so that you won't have resentment about that person.

So, you should always do something from the kindness of your heart, and if you can't do that, then you should say no. You should try to put yourself first because while you want to do something for somebody else, you should know if that thing is going to be good for you too.

Stand Your Ground

Now the next one is to stand your ground. This is the hardest situation to be in because you are not used to enforcing your boundaries with people. You are not used to standing up for yourself. So, once you know what you want, then telling somebody no, might be uncomfortable for you because you have never done it before, but standing your ground is acknowledging that what you are doing is best for you and no one else. It won't make you a bad person, and it won't make you a selfish friend or anything like that, but it would only mean that you love yourself, and you tend to put yourself first.

You should know that you don't need to explain yourself in a detailed explanation as to why the answer is no. Simply telling somebody, "No, I cannot" with a brief explanation is all you need. Anybody that loves you will respect the fact that your answer is no. But somebody that is manipulative or has a fragile ego or does not love you is going to backlash you. So, before the manipulation starts, the guilt may come and then the shame, and then when it doesn't work for them their real abusive behavior comes into play.

Be Prepared For Backlash

The next one is to be prepared for backlash. This is the part that the person will tell you that you are selfish and he always does things for you, but you never do things back for him and why would he even have someone like you in his life, and all he is asking from you is simple favor, and you turned him down. He may start bullying you or start threatening you, and he will say something like, "I'm never going to do anything for you again." So, he will use a lot of things to throw you off your game. Just expect it to come your way so that you will know how to handle it. You shouldn't get angry or defensive with the person but you should see the person as who they are, and just sit back and stay in your truth on what you want and say no to them and only say "I'm sorry you feel that way."

That is one of the best things to say to a manipulated person because after you have seen it, the person won't really have anything again. After all, you are acknowledging that they feel a certain way, and you are sorry that they feel the way they feel. Now you have to remember that all these things are going to take a lot of time. It is going to take a lot of practice on your part, and it will take time for the people around you to get used to it, but the more you continue to love yourself, the more it will become easier for you.

Cut Them Off

So, what you should do is to take a scaffold and cut that person out of your life like the way you will cut down a tree. This is what you should do because of the sponge mind effect that your mind has.

It tends to soak everything off because of the averaging law. Once negativity steps into your system, it builds up, and it grows like cancer and starts spreading throughout your whole body and through your mind. Moreover, eventually, it will start affecting your habit, affect your way of thinking, and colors your perspective of the world.

So, this can be very dangerous if it is happening over a long time, so you have to build the courage to cut these people out of your life. One thing that you have to acknowledge to yourself is that it doesn't matter who that person is. If somebody is violating your standards and your principles in life, then that person should be cut out of your life. It doesn't matter who it is, whether he's your boss, or your co-workers, or your friends, or your customers. You can cut them out of your life. You could even cut your family out of your life. Most people have problems with their family, and they feel like they can't cut out their family out of their life. Or they feel like they have a very good old friend from Middle School that they have known for decades and they can't cut him. Or they can't cut a client because it's a really important client, and they can't cut their boss off from their work.

So, they give out so many excuses for who they can and cannot cut and why there are certain people in their lives that they cannot cut off. You have to accept that everybody can be cut out of your life. You need to have boundaries, and you need to have principles as a human being. You hold onto yourself to keep those principles, and you hold onto other people to keep those principles. Now, this doesn't mean that you have to be like a stickler and just cut somebody off for any stupid reason.

It only means that when somebody violates your rules, you can cut them out of your life. Now the closer the person is to you and the more important they are, the more leeway that you can give them. These are people like your mum, your dad, your brother, your sister, or your children. You still need to have boundaries because if you don't set boundaries subconsciously, they will realize that you have no boundaries and people that are close to you will be looking for what they can get away with, and they will keep getting away with more and more things.

So, these toxic people are not really self-developed. They are not operating from a high place of consciousness; they are just running their life like an animal. They have a very animalistic lifestyle, they have low consciousness, and they are just doing the easiest things in life. And those types of people, tend to demand more out of life from you. They tend to be a bigger drag. So, for those types of people, you need to set boundaries.

So right now, you have to acknowledge to yourself that there are some circumstances may demand that you can cut off anybody no matter how close the person may be, to you. A family member, who is toxic, may be cut off only as the last resort. As for other people, you should have fewer reservations to cut. Now you should cut somebody out of your life depending on the type of person, their closeness to you, and how important they are to you. You should sit down with the person and tell them the problem that you have with them and tell them that it is over between you two and that there should be no contact between the two of you and then just draw a line. You can simply delete the person's number if the person is a casual acquaintance. Don't contact them anymore, block their numbers, block their emails, and block whatever means of communication that you were using to communicate with them, or just stop responding to them. If you are in a relationship like an intimate relationship, then break up with that person.

Breaking up is tough, but sometimes you have to deal with it. If you're in a marriage and the other person is toxic, then consider going for a divorce. Now that may be a nasty process, but it is better than sitting in a toxic marriage for 10 or 20 years. You will not be able to sit in that kind of relationship for a long time. So, you should cut the marriage off so that it will not get worse than it is.

If it is in your career, consider quitting your job, or change your job or move to a different department or do a different type of job in the company. If you are the boss or you are self-employed and you have toxic employees, then you can consider firing them. If you have contracts with bad customers, then cut off those contracts and say no to them even if they are going to bring you more clients.

And if the worst comes to the worst and you are in a negative environment, or you are in a really bad part of the city, or you are living in a bad part of the State, or you are living in a toxic country, then consider relocating. If the worst comes to the worst, you could go to a new city or go to a new country. You need to do that because your environment is very influential on the kind of life that you have and the kind of emotions that you will feel, and the kind of success that you will get. So, take this thing seriously. Now you don't need to cut everybody from your life. Sometimes you might just need to do a reformation. If somebody is violating your values and you are fed up with all the toxicity, you can sit down with that person and tell the person what your boundaries and expectations are. Now, this is going to be a difficult task, but you should have that talk and see what happens. Sometimes the talk will change the person, and the person will say, "I didn't even realize that I was hurting you so badly, and I don't even realize that I was messing your life up with my toxicity or my negativity; let me see if I can change something". Sometimes, they will do that because they value the relationship, and they know that you will cut them off from your life if they don't. Sometimes some of the people in a low conscious state that can't help themselves may be addicted to drugs or maybe they are depressed, or they have a lot of bad habits, or they don't want to change and they don't care about changing. This could be the most common cause because these people don't care, they don't want to change and they are not going to accommodate you, so they are going to keep repeating and violating your values, and they won't listen to you, even if you talk to them. They will just continue running on autopilot and be breaking your boundaries.

CHAPTER 9:

How Not To Be Manipulated

How To Defend Yourself From Manipulators

At the end of the day, we are indeed humans. It's precisely because of this that we get to dwell on the view of others in everything we do. We always want and love validation from others so we can subconsciously decide whether or not we will be depressed. In this millennial age, the norm has been just bragging about their wealth in social media. Many of these bragging are often the reality but in the end, this leads to a loose connection with reality. This kind of self-deception can dig deep into the human system, and one day a victim of this may wake up and realize that only in her servant's eye does her perfect world exist. Depression will follow suit tightly. The first step towards protecting yourself against persuasion and manipulation is to confront the scenario and to take the position of disrupting any illusions. You won't be able to go through your lives usually. You must be careful that you regulate your own decisions and then consciously decide to see stuff for what they really are. This agreement, which seems too good to be true, could actually be true. The other thing you should do is trust your instincts certainly. Sometimes you have been told a lie in the most competent manner that you can believe. But at a specific instinctive rate, you can feel an imbalance between what should, what is, and then what is projected on you. There might be no physical sign that something is wrong, but you think that something is wrong. The next significant thing when you ask questions is to hear the answers. This can sound unbelievable because you're going to listen to the responses. The reality is that we can deceive ourselves by choosing the responses we receive. We say that we look, but we only care about the reactions that we want to hear and not the answers that we receive. You may have broken your illusions, but some of you still hold on to the comfort of those illusions. You would not hear the real answers to your questions because of the pain that comes with handling the scenario. Actual hearing needs a certain feeling of detachment, but not reality this time around.

You must get rid of your feelings. Your detachment from your emotions would lead you to the next step in processing the new data logically. It can make situations more complicated than they have to be. It makes it so hard for your exit strategy, to allow all feelings to cool down and spring. The irrational part of you may want to let everything go to hell when you face reality. Your justified anger can encourage you to take short-term measures to calm your feelings. But you may come to regret these actions in the long term. I'm not saying that you should deny your emotions; I'm not saying that you do not act on these emotions. First, deal with the situations and later deal with your emotions.

Act Fast

It's lovely that you have got to grips with the truth of things. But it is so much more to defend ourselves against these dark, manipulative strategies. While you try to protect yourself against the claws of these manipulators, it is often intense and exciting at first. The intensity of these feelings can slowly lead to negation. The longer you take any action, the quicker the denial will begin, and if it occurs, there is a strong likelihood that you may fall back and end up being trapped on the same internet. You can avoid this by taking action as soon as you know someone is attempting to manipulate you. This can be done in the most natural way possible, as when informing a close friend about some facts of the specific scenario, all the events that will eventually lead you to liberty can be so started. You should understand that after choosing to behave, the fabric is made of sturdier material than glass. The illusion can work its way back to your core by using fragmented parts of your feelings to solve it. When a liar is caught in a lie, you may try to hire others to implement that lying if they think they no longer hold you. A disappointing partner with whom you broke stuff lately would attempt to use the other shared links in your lives to change your mind. You are going to need both your logic and instincts if you want to get out of this unscathed. While the reality is that when you find that you have always been lied to, you get emotionally scarred, so you are still left untouched by the scenario. However, priority should be provided to follow the path that enables you to go to this toxic condition without further harm. You're mentally all over the location. Rage, rage, hurt, and disappointment are the tip of the iceberg. But you must logically believe. Keep your head above the water and warn yourself.

Get Assistance Quickly

When you are trapped in the manipulations of others, confusion is one of the feelings you would encounter. This will obscure your rational thinking and make you feel helpless. You could even question the truth of what you're currently facing. If you continue to have those doubts, it will lead to denial. You will likely want to say that you have the whole scenario wrong. You misunderstood specific stuff and came to the incorrect conclusion. Such thinking would lead back to the weapons of the manipulator. Resist the desire to accept a second opinion. In a health crisis, people go to another physician to get a second view. This is to clear any doubts about your first diagnosis and to confirm the best course of therapy for you.

Similarly, receiving an opinion from another person can assist you in discerning reality and your next steps. Just remember, it's better to go to someone who's proven to have your best interest at heart many times. The next step, is to confront the perpetrator if you have the assistance that you need. I recommend you choose the scene or place for this. Select a location that provides you the upper hand. That would involve some cautious planning on your part. If the offender exists in the cyber world, especially if you have been swindled by the person, you must engage the police and the authorities concerned. Do some of your research to find out the truth. After you face the offender and take the measures you need to get out of the scenario, the healing method must begin rapidly. The extent and severity you have been harmed, manipulated, or abused do not matter. You have to be able to go through it and wait for your wounds to be "healed," rather than sitting on your bed and living the past.

Time would offer you sufficient distance from your experience, but you would seldom be healing from emotional scars if you learned something about this book. If you don't do anything, an unhealthy scab might form over the wound that makes you vulnerable, if not more than you have experienced. Speak to a consultant, take part in the treatment, and actively facilitate the healing process, regardless of what you choose. It will not occur overnight, but you are sure you get nearer each day with every phase of your treatment.

Have Confidence in Your Instincts

While your brain interprets signals based on facts, logic, and experience, it operates in the opposite direction by filtering data through an emotional filter. The only thing that takes vibrations is your intestine that cannot pick up either the heart or the brain. If you can groom up to the stage where you acknowledge your inner voice and are trained to do so, you will reduce your likelihood of becoming seduced by individuals who try to manipulate you. It's difficult to acknowledge this voice at first, and this is because we have permitted sounds of doubt, self-discrimination, and the loud voices of the critics within and without drowning our authentic voices in our lives. This voice or instinct relies on your survival. So, trust that your brain cells will still be able to process stuff in your immediate area when it starts. Some individuals call it intuition, some call it instinct, and they do the same, particularly when it comes to relationships. You must acknowledge that starting to trust your instincts may not always make logical sense. If you've ever been doing something and felt like you were suddenly watched, then you understand what I mean.

You have no eyes at the rear of your head, nobody else in the space, but you have the small shiver running down the back of your neck, and you're looking at the "sudden understanding" , that is what I am talking about. I am talking about that. The first step in connecting with your instinct is to decode your mind with your voices. You can do this with meditation. Forget about chatting concentrate on your middle. You're the voice that you understand. Next, be attentive to your ideas. Don't just throw away your head's eclectic monologs. Instead, go with the stream of thoughts.

Why do you believe in somebody somehow? How do you feel so deeply, even though you knew each other for only a few days? What's this nagging feeling about this other individual? You become more sensitive to your intuition as you explore your ideas and know when your instincts start and respond to them. You might have to learn to stop and believe if you are the individual who, at present, wants to make stimulating choices. This break provides you the chance to reflect and assess your options. The next part is hard, and many people can't follow it. You can't sail or navigate this step, unfortunately. You need to be open to the concept of self-confidence and trusting others to believe in your instinct. Your lack of confidence would only make you paranoid, and when you're paranoid, it's not your instincts that kick. It's your fear! Every molehill tends to transform fear into a mountain. You have to let go of your concern, embrace trust, and make your fresh relationships lead. You can hear the voice better without the roadblocks of fear in your mind. Finally, your priorities must be reassessed.

You may not see the past if your mind is at the forefront of money and material property. Any contact you have with individuals would be viewed as individuals who try to use you, and it will quickly become truth if you live like this very often. Let's understand that we draw what we believe in, to your lives. If you always think about material wealth, you will only attract individuals like yourself. Look at your interactions with this new view with this guide; the old, the new, and the outlook. Don't enter into a partnership you expect to play. Be accessible to them, whether it is a company relationship, a romantic relationship, or even a regular knowledge. You can receive the correct feedback from your intuition. Do not think this too that, if you encounter suspects, your gut will tell you to go in the opposite direction.

CHAPTER 10:

Behavioral Traits Of Favorite Victims Of Manipulators

There are certain characteristics and behavioral traits that make people more vulnerable to manipulation and people with dark psychology traits know this fully well. They tend to seek out victims who have those specific behavioral traits because they are essentially easy targets. Let's discuss six of the traits of the favorite victims of manipulators.

Emotional Insecurity And Fragility

Manipulators like to target victims who are emotionally insecure or emotionally fragile. Unfortunately for these victims, such traits are very easy to identify even in total strangers, so it's easy for experienced manipulators to find them.

People who are emotionally insecure tend to be very defensive when they are attacked or when they are under pressure and that makes them easy to spot in social situations. Even after just a few interactions, a manipulator can gauge with a certain degree of accuracy, how insecure a person is. They'll try to provoke their potential targets in a subtle way, and then wait to see how the target reacts. If they are overly defensive, manipulators will take it as a sign of insecurity, and they will intensify their manipulative attacks.

Manipulators can also tell if a target is emotionally insecure if he/she redirects accusations or negative comments. They will find a way to put you on the spot, and if you try to throw it back at them, or to make excuses instead of confronting the situation head-on, the manipulator could conclude that you are insecure and therefore an easy target.

People who have social anxiety also tend to have emotional insecurity, and manipulators are aware of this fact. In social gatherings, they can easily spot individuals who have social anxiety, then target them for manipulation. "Pickup artists" are able to identify the girls who seem uneasy in social situations by the way they conduct themselves. Social anxiety is difficult to conceal, especially to manipulators who are experienced at preying on emotional vulnerability.

Emotional fragility is different from emotional insecurity. Emotionally insecure people tend to show it all the time, while emotionally fragile people appear to be normal, but they break down emotionally at the slightest provocation. Manipulators like targeting emotionally fragile people because it's very easy to elicit a reaction from them. Once a manipulator finds out that you are emotionally fragile, he is going to jump at any chance of manipulating you because he knows it would be fairly easy.

Emotional fragility can be temporary, so people with these traits are often targeted by opportunistic manipulators.

A person may be emotionally stable most of the time, but he/she may experience emotional fragility when they are going through a breakup, when they are grieving, or when they are dealing with a situation that is emotionally draining, the more diabolical manipulators can earn your trust, bid their time, and wait for you to be emotionally fragile.

Alternatively, they can use underhanded methods to induce emotional fragility in a person they are targeting.

Sensitive People

Highly sensitive people are those individuals who process information at a deeper level and are more aware of the subtleties in social dynamics. They have lots of positive attributes because they tend to be very considerate of others, and they watch their step to avoid causing people any harm, whether directly or indirectly. Such people tend to dislike any form of violence or cruelty, and they are easily upset by news reports about disastrous occurrences, or even depictions of gory scenes in movies.

Sensitive people also tend to get emotionally exhausted from taking in other people's feelings. When they walk into a room, they have the immediate ability to detect other people's moods, because they are naturally skilled at identifying and interpreting other people's body language cues, facial expressions, and tonal variations.

Manipulators like to target sensitive people because they are easy to manipulate. If you are sensitive to certain things, manipulators can use them against you. They will feign certain emotions to draw sensitive people in so that they can exploit them.

Sensitive people also tend to scare easily. They have a heightened "startle reflex," which means that they are more likely to show clear signs of fear or nervousness in potentially threatening situations. For example, sensitive people are more likely to jump up when someone sneaks up on them, even before they determine whether they are in any real danger. If you are a sensitive person, this trait can be very difficult to hide, and malicious people will be able to see it from a mile away.

Sensitive people also tend to be withdrawn. They are mostly introverts, and they like to keep to themselves because social stimulation can be emotionally draining for them. Manipulators who are looking to control others are more likely to target people who are introverted because that trait makes it easy to isolate potential victims.

Manipulators can also identify sensitive people by listening to how they talk. Sensitive people tend to be very proper; they never use vulgar language, and they tend to be very politically correct because they are trying to avoid offending anyone. They also tend to be polite, and they say please and thank you more often than others. Manipulators go after such people because they know that they are too polite to dismiss them right away; sensitive people will indulge anyone because they don't want to be rude, and that gives maliciously people a way in.

Empathic People

Empathic people are generally similar to highly sensitive people, except that they are more attuned to the feelings of others and the energy of the world around them. They tend to internalize other people's suffering to the point that it becomes their own. In fact, for some of them, it can be difficult to distinguish someone's discomfort from their own. Empathic people make the best partners because they feel everything you feel. However, this makes them particularly easy to manipulate, which is why malicious people like to target them.

Malicious people can feign certain emotions, and convey those emotions to emphatic people, who will feel them as though they were real. That opens them up for exploitation. Empathic people are the favorite targets of psychopathic con men because they feel so deeply for others. A con man can make up stories about financial difficulties and swindle lots of money from empathic people.

The problem with being empathic is that because you have such strong emotions, you easily dismiss your own doubts about people because you would much rather offer help to a person who turns out to be a liar than deny help to a person who turns out to be telling the truth.

Empathic people have a big-hearts, and they tend to be extremely generous often to their own detriment. They are highly charitable, and they feel guilty when others around them suffer, even if it's not their fault and they can't do anything about it. Malicious people have a very easy time taking such people on guilt trips. They are the kind of people who would willingly fork over their life savings to help their friends get out of debt, even if it means they would be ruined financially.

Malicious people like to get into relationships with emphatic people because they are easy to take advantage of. Empathic people try to avoid getting into intimate relationships in the first place because they know that it's easy for them to get engulfed in such relationships and to lose their identities in the process. However, manipulators will doggedly pursue them because they know that once they get it, they can guilt the empathic person into doing anything they want.

Fear Of Loneliness

Many people are afraid of being alone, but this fear is more heightened in a small percentage of the population. This kind of fear can be truly paralyzing for those who experience it, and it can open them up to exploitation by malicious people. For example, there are many people who stay in dysfunctional relationships because they are afraid that they might never find someone else to love them if they break up with an abusive partner. Manipulators can identify this fear in a victim, and they'll often do everything they can to fuel it further to make sure that the person is crippled by it. People who are afraid of being alone can tolerate or even rationalize any kind of abuse.

The fear of being alone can be easy to spot in a potential victim. People with this kind of fear tend to exude some level of desperation at the beginning of relationships, and they can sometimes come across as clingy. While ordinary people may think of being clingy as a red flag, manipulative people will see it as an opportunity to exploit somebody. If you are attached to them, they'll use manipulative techniques to make you even more dependent on them. They can withhold love and affection (e.g., by using the silent treatment) to make the victim fear that he/she is about to get dumped so that they act out of desperation and cede more control to the manipulator.

The fear of being alone is for the most part a social construct, and it disproportionately affects women more than men. For generations, our society has taught women that their goal in life is to get married and have children, so, even the more progressive women who reject this social construct are still plagued by social pressures to adhere to those old standards. That being said, men also tend to be afraid of being alone.

People with abandonment issues stemming from childhood tend to experience the fear of loneliness to a higher degree. There are also those people who may not necessarily fear loneliness in general, but they are afraid of being separated from the important people in their lives.

For example, lots of people end up staying in abusive or dysfunctional relationships because they are afraid of being separated from their children.

Fear Of Disappointing Others

We all feel a certain sense of obligation towards the people in our lives, but there are some people who are extremely afraid of disappointing others. This kind of fear is similar to the fear of embarrassment and the fear of rejection because it means that the person puts a lot of stock into how others perceive him or her.

The fear of disappointing others can occur naturally, and it can actually be useful in some situations; parents who are afraid of disappointing their families will work harder to provide for them, and children who are afraid of disappointing their parents will study harder at school. In this case, the fear is actually constructive.

However, it becomes unhealthy when it's directed at the wrong people, or when it forces you to compromise your own comfort and happiness.

When manipulators find out that you have a fear of disappointing others, they'll try to put you in a position where you feel like you owe them something. They'll do certain favors for you, and then they'll manipulate you into believing that you have a sense of obligation towards them. They will then guilt you into complying with any request whenever they want something from you.

Personality Dependent Disorders And Emotional Dependency

Dependent personality disorder refers to a real disorder that is characterized by a person having an excessive and even pervasive need to be taken care of. This need often leads the person to become submissive towards the people in their lives and to be clingy and afraid of separation. People with this disorder act in ways that are meant to elicit caregiving. They tend to practice what's called "learned helplessness." This is where they act out of a conviction that they are unable to do certain things for themselves, and they need the help of others.

Such people have a hard time making decisions, even when dealing with simple things like picking out which clothes to wear. They need constant reassurance and advice, and they let others take the lead in their own lives. These are the kinds of people who either move back into their parents' homes as adults or treat their spouses and partners as though they are their parents.

Manipulators like to target people with dependent personality disorders because they are very easy to control and dominate. These people willingly cede control over their lives to others, so when manipulators come knocking, they don't face much resistance. Manipulators start off by giving them a false sense of security, but once they have won their trust, they switch gears and start imposing their will on them.

Emotional dependency is somewhat similar to dependent personality disorder, but it doesn't rise to the level of clinical significance. It stems from having low self-esteem, and it's often a result of childhood abandonment issues. People with an emotional dependency will play the submissive role in relationships for fear of losing their partners. They tend to be very agreeable because they want to please the people in their lives. Such people are easy to manipulate, and malicious people can easily dominate them.

126

CHAPTER 11:

How To Read And Analyze People

How to Read People

The ability to read people have more to do with nonverbal communication and body language alone. The essential things to look at before you can successfully read people include posture, gestures, physical movements, the person's appearance, facial expressions, the tone of voice and willingness to make eye contact during conversations etc. There is a study that finds that you can read someone only 7% from the words they say, 38% from their vocal clue, such as tone, pitch and volume and finally, 55% from their body language. The study was however focused on reading someone on a first impression basis.

You also have to consider the context in which the behaviors are being exhibited, personally and the possibility that anybody might try to deceive you by manipulating the communication.

Establish a baseline

Majority of people have different behavioral quirks and sometimes these quirks are habitual. Examples include clearing their throat, scratching their head, stroking their necks and so on. It is, however, essential that you read and understand what the normal behavior of the person is, and that would be your baseline.

Know the person: In order to be able to read a person better, you have to establish a baseline and to establish a baseline; you have to know the person well. By getting to know them personally, you are going to have a better idea of the things they like and do not like, their behavioral habits etc. Also, you have to pay attention to the individuals and their habits, even the littlest habits, such as eye gaze, fluttering the eyes etc. This will help you in noting the things to look for when you are analyzing them.

Ask open-ended questions: During the process of reading someone, what you are doing is watching and listening. What you are not doing however, is taking control of the conversation and steering it in your direction. Ask your questions straight and make your conclusions. Open-ended questions will give the individual room to talk more, allowing you to observe them for a longer time. When you ask questions that are not straight to the point, you may get a rambling reply that may not provide you with adequate information.

Look for inconsistencies in their baseline. It is also important to seek out the discrepancies in the baseline. For instance, when a normally affectionate person turns out to not be physically present anymore and does not seem to want to be close to anyone, then you should know that something is up with such person.

Work in Clusters: Identifying only one cue is not enough reason to make conclusions. For instance, someone could lean away from you because the chair on which they are sitting is hard to be comfortable in. Even if you are focused on their nonverbal behavior, make sure to identify between three and four different signs before you make conclusions.

You can take a cue from their tone, their body, their face, and their words. If you can get one from each, then it may be safe to make assumptions.

Identify your own weaknesses. "It is the nature of man to err." This statement indicates the vulnerability of humans and their fallibility. Everybody likes pretty things, even the Pope, and the odds are when you identify something as pretty, you are going to like it, even if the "pretty" thing is dangerous.

How to Analyze People

The ability to analyze the people around you can help you determine their true motives. It can be very difficult to read people and, let's face it; some people are excellent at covering up the truth. Nefarious plots and schemes can be seen in your everyday life. Whether you are at work, at home, or out with friends we are sure you deal with people constantly who are trying to manipulate you in one way or another. Putting time into understanding Dark Psychology can make seeing these truths about people and their intent infinitely easier. It truly does play a critical role in your ability to lead your best life.

Staying protected from people that have dark tendencies is important, especially in your work life. We have all had a job at one time or another that was ruled by drill sergeants.

Those people that believe you build a team through fear and intimidation. Conversely, you may have had a manager that treated everyone well but realistically relied on covert scare tactics and manipulation to hold on to power and control.

Typically, we see more of these types of tendencies in upper management. People that focus solely on being the boss, are oftentimes, more apt to succumb to the dark pieces of human nature. They are willing to do some deplorable things to gain power, such as using intimidation tactics. Why would they work hard and fair to gain power when they can simply lie, manipulate, and deceive people to get what they want quickly?

You may have also experienced the co-worker that is never happy with other people's success. The person that starts to spread rumors about you simply because you are doing well. They try to turn people, including the management, against you so that you will fall and they will succeed. Sometimes the way these people behave is very petty. Using small verbal digs to make you feel inferior. This can throw you off of your work game and ultimately lead to a loss of your job in more extreme cases.

Employees that are arrogant, quick to anger, condescending, or domineering can truly rip a team apart. Being assertive and nipping their annoying and detrimental behaviors in the bud can help to ensure your team stays focused and cohesive. You can also work on being aware of people's body language and use empathy to ease a troubling situation.

Managing your own emotions can also help you keep a cool head and ward off any unnecessary tendencies before they become a problem. In addition, being in control of yourself can help you observe the actions that are happening around you as it is easier to have a broader perspective. Mastering these techniques takes time but can save you a lot of drama in your workplace.

When you have the ability to pick out the traits of these types of people, it can help you deal with the repercussion. Instead of feeling weak and vulnerable you will feel empowered. No longer allowing people to make you feel small or cause detriment to your career is quite freeing. Keep in mind that dealing with people that succumb to our darker sides can be very difficult.

It is truly important when learning about traits like cheating, manipulation, lying, and selfishness that we look in the mirror. Self-actualization is an important factor of living your best life and being a good person. So, looking at your habits and pinpointing the ones that are detrimental to those around you is important. Even more importantly is figuring out how to change them so that you can evolve into something better.

Finding the flaws in ourselves can be difficult. Broadening your perspective so you can see the things you do is even harder. With time and effort, however, you can truly work on these negative internal aspects to improve yourself. This is not only good for you but also for the people you come in contact with on a daily basis.

Having bad habits is part of life. Sometimes, these habits are simply annoying; like chewing with your mouth open. Other times, it is devastating to our lives. A good example of this is telling lies to spare feelings or to stop you from some sort of trouble. Other excellent examples are doing things like flattering people to get your way and being extremely cynical of other people's thoughts or beliefs.

Having the realization that you are doing these things does not come easy for many people. It can take a lot of hard work and dedication to truly find the ability to improve the way that you act and change your bad habits. There are a variety of ways that people have implemented to help aid them in finding their true self and dealing with their less than stellar qualities.

134

CHAPTER 12:

Micro Expressions and Body Language – A Basic Primer

Imagine if you could 'read' body languages to an extent where you knew exactly what someone was expressing, despite the actual words that they were telling you. This is actually something you that you can do to an extent. Let's talk about micro expressions. Popularized largely by a show entitled 'Lie to me', this focused on the fictional life of Dr.Cal Lightman. 'Lie to Me' was the story of a behavioral specialist who, could tell if someone was lying based on facial tics and would let the doctor know if someone was lying or otherwise engaged in deceit.

The science from the show is surprisingly 90% accurate but, while they cannot tell you if someone is actually lying, they can give you a very good idea if someone is experiencing emotions contrary to the story that they are telling. So, how accurate is the science? It's accurate enough that it is taught to the FBI and the U.S. Secret Service. First discovered in 1966 by Dr. Isaacs and Dr.Haggard. Micro expressions gained popularity later with the research of Dr. Paul Ekman. Reviewing many skills of psychiatric sessions, Dr. Ekman was able to discern 7 different emotions that were present, despite the language or culture of the individual being reviewed. Fascinating? No? We're going to go a little into micro expressions and then further into common body language vs. culturally influenced body language in order to enable you have a better understanding on how to deal with practitioners of dark psychology.

These are actually just indicators of the presence of feelings rather than actual proof of deceit; it is still a fascinating science which can be useful to you – 7 different universal factors that you can see clearly on someone's face if you know what you are looking for. Even a seasoned dark psychologist can't hide the emotions if you know where to look.

The 7 emotional factors (which show regardless of your linguistic or cultural background) are as follows:

Happiness - Lip-corners are turned up. Wrinkling (crow's feet) at the sides of the eyes are present, along with a raising of the cheeks.

Anger - Lips are pressed tightly together. A widening of the eyes and lowering of the eyebrows into the middle of the forehead occur as well.

Sadness - Lip-corners are turned down. Eyebrows angled, close together and raised.

Fear - A widening of the eyes and raising of the eyebrows occurring with slow opening and widening of the mouth. Upper eyelids will be pulled up/in.

Surprise - Similar to fear, an open mouth with a widening of the eyes (the pupils will dilate as well) and raised eyebrows.

Disgust - Wrinkling of the nose and a raised upper lip, with lips loosely displayed.

Contempt - Head goes slightly back and one side of the lips is raised.

These are just some quick examples in what is a very rich subject. Any of the books by Dr. Paul Ekman are good for research on this, as well as a quick Google. A number of the sites display facial examples in order to help you to familiarize yourself with the different expressions in order to apply them for your own use, and there are even a number of video courses on this for you to learn better

Aside from micro expressions, many body language expressions can be useful to learn when determining if someone may be sending you mixed messages, either consciously or subconsciously.

Let's review some nonverbal cues that you see daily and talk about their most common meanings. Learning these cues can help you to better determine if the words that someone is saying to you match what their body language is telling you. Remember, nonverbal cues are not a 100% foolproof of reading intentions, but they can be very, very useful to you. Some have been mentioned before, but we have collected a list in this chapter in order to place them with other cues that you may also look for. Be sure to look for as many of these cues in the next few days to see how common they are. They are an excellent tool in avoiding becoming a victim of dark psychology.

Nonverbal Cues Associated with Sitting:

Nonverbal cue: Someone sitting with legs crossed with foot kicking slightly up and down.

Often indicates: This one we've all done. It typically indicates boredom and a little impatience (although the latter is not guaranteed, as many of us do it without thinking). Not generally something to worry about unless someone claims to have great interest in what you are saying at the time.

Nonverbal cue: Sitting with legs apart comfortably.

Often indicates: Generally something you'll see men do most of the time. This is indicative that the person is relaxed and comfortable with your presence.

Nonverbal cue: Their ankles are locked together while sitting.

Often indicates: This one typically indicates a state of apprehension or nervousness.

If combined with some of the other worry expressions here, it could mean that they have some bad news for you or are worried about your reaction to something.

Nonverbal Cues Associated with Arms:

Nonverbal cue: Arms crossed over the chest.

Often indicates: Unless it's cold out, this is typically a defensive posture. You won't see it so often with figures of authority who tend to display arms comfortably at their sides, or perhaps with a hand in one pocket to indicate ease.

Nonverbal cue: Complete stillness of the arms in conversation.

Often indicates: This is one to watch for, as stillness of the arms can indicate purposeful masking of body language or tenseness at the very least. Proceed with caution.

Nonverbal cue: The gripping of one's own arm.

Often indicates: Gripping one's own arms is a gesture of self-comfort with typically negative connotations. You'll see this one a lot when people are waiting in a government office to renew a license and the wait is long, on airplanes from those with a fear of flying, or quite commonly, in doctors' offices.

Nonverbal cue: Their arms and hands are held low in front of them, with hands clasped.

Often indicates: This is a position of defense and can indicate that the subject is feeling vulnerable or otherwise insecure about their position in the conversation. Keep in mind that dark psychology practitioners are also aware of this and may adopt this stance to appear more vulnerable. You see this pose adopted often when people are asking for help.

Nonverbal Expressions Associated with Fingers and Hand Gestures:

Nonverbal cue: They have their hand resting on their cheek.

Often indicates: This can indicate that someone is thinking or perhaps evaluating the situation.

Nonverbal cue: Touching the nose or scratching the nose.

Often indicates: This can indicate disbelief or, in some cases, may indicate that the person is deceiving you. Watch for how they do it. Usually, a genuine scratch is going to be quick and efficient. If it is occurring a lot and it's not cold season, then this may be a nonverbal cue to watch for.

Nonverbal cue: Someone is rubbing one eye while you are speaking.

Often indicates: This is another indicator that someone may not believe what you are saying. Take the weather in consideration and, if the rubbing of the eye seems a bit fishy, then note it to yourself.

Nonverbal cue: Someone approaches with their hands clasped behind their back.

Often indicates: This can indicate frustration, irritation, and anger in many cases. It is sometimes adopted as a domination posture in the workplace, as well as a way of showing aggression.

Nonverbal cue: Someone has their head resting in one hand and their eyes looking down.

Often indicates: This one typically just indicates that the subject is bored.

Nonverbal cue: Someone is sitting with their hands clasped behind their head and with their legs crossed.

Often indicates: Confidence, superiority.

Nonverbal cue: Someone is steepling their fingers while speaking to you.

Often indicates: This is typically a gesture of authority where the person that you are speaking with feels they are the dominant presence.

Nonverbal cue: Someone presents open palms when they see you.

Often indicates: This is a gesture meant to show sincerity and to inspire openness in a conversation. It is also a way of communicating symbolically 'I have no weapons in my hands, you can trust me.'

Nonverbal cue: Someone pinches the bridge of their nose, closing their eyes momentarily.

Often indicates: This generally indicates that someone is responding negatively to the subject at hand.

Nonverbal cue: Someone is drumming their fingers on the table or tapping.

Often indicates: This is something we've all seen and merely indicative of impatience.

Nonverbal cue: Someone is playing with their hair.

Often indicates: If this behavior is not in an atmosphere conducive to flirting, then it can indicate that the person is feeling insecure.

Nonverbal cue: Someone is moving around excessively.

Often indicates: If someone you are speaking with is playing with their pencil, tapping their feet, or playing in their chair, basically any excessive movement as if distracted, is a common indicator of impatience.

Nonverbal cue: Someone is stroking their chin.

Often indicates: This is commonly associated as an evaluation gesture and indicates that someone is coming to a decision.

Nonverbal Gestures of the Head:

Nonverbal cue: Someone quickly tilts their head slightly during a conversation.

Often indicates: This is an indicator that what you have just said or something they have noticed in the environment has suddenly gotten their attention. It is always a good thing to notice when leading a conversation or ascertaining motives.

Nonverbal cue: Lowering of the head in conversation.

Often indicates: There are a number of meanings to this depending on a few factors. For instance, a quick lowering of the head is a mini-nod, indicative of an agreement or feigned agreement. If eye contact is maintained, it can be a sign of flirtation or an indication of distrust, depending on the context. If lowering the head so that the chin is covering the neck, then it is a defensive gesture. It can also indicate frustration or exhaustion, although, in such cases, it is often followed with a sigh.

Nonverbal cue: Their head is perfectly still while speaking to you.

Often indicates: This can indicate that the person is serious or feels they are speaking from a position dominant/in authority of you. This can also be indicative of anger or potential violence.

Miscellaneous Nonverbal Cues

Nonverbal cue: Invading personal space.

Often indicates: Typically a distance of one foot is reserved for family and friends so, if someone you barely know is doing this, you should be on the lookout. Four feet is the typical comfort distance for personal space in most countries.

Nonverbal cue: Body-language mirroring.

Often indicates: Be careful. The person might be doing this unconsciously, as mirrored body language tends to put the recipient at ease; however, this can also be a conscious attempt to put you in the same state. Be wary of this one.

Nonverbal cue: Object barriers.

Often indicates: This is done most often subconsciously and represents the act of putting a barrier between them and yourself. This is typically a means of avoiding showing your insecurities to someone. The next time you are in a bar or a similar public venue, take a look around and you'll see people doing it, usually with their glasses clasped in both hands in front of them.

Now that we have gone a through a number of nonverbal cues, it is worth noting that there are some cues that you may never see due to cultural differences. For instance, closer proximity is considered aggressive in Japan. Constant eye contact also makes people very uncomfortable, whereas in Spanish and Arabic cultures, NOT maintaining a lot of eye contact is considered very disrespectful. For the majority of the nonverbal cues here, however, you shouldn't have any problems, just be sure to do a little research if you like to travel so that you don't misinterpret a cue if you intend to go somewhere exotic.

Now that we have given you a larger sampling of the information that you need, you will want to practice it. As mentioned at the beginning of this chapter, take a week looking for nonverbal cues, such as you have read in this chapter, to see how many of them that you can identify. You will find a number of them readily in the workplace and at social venues that you frequent. Use this information to better arm yourself for dealing with dark psychology. Knowing them may not guarantee that you will be immune to being manipulated, surely not, but not knowing them will most certainly guarantee to make you less likely not to notice them when you should be on your guard. Arm yourself as best you can with this information, it's the good stuff!

CHAPTER 13:

The Framework of Dark Psychology

A framework, within all realms of science, is a structured approach consisting of separate sectors that support a theoretical study or research. Within the broad range of popular psychology, there is a theoretical framework consisting of five points and a psychological framework used in general psychiatric practice. Both of these things are applied to Dark Psychology. The theoretical framework is altered very little in dark psychiatric works while the psychological framework varies in relation to the type of work being performed (treatment or study). The theoretical framework consists of Structure, Function, Behavior, Cognitive Ability, and Psychoanalysis.

- *Structuralism-* This entity of the psychological theoretical framework is implemented every time. The goal is to identify the specific points of the patient's psychological experiences using a technique called introspection. Introspection was developed by psychologist Wilhelm Wundt and relies on the patient's own reflection of their internal emotions and thoughts. These thoughts and feelings are then processed into the most basic forms of consciousness.

- *Functionalism-* Functionalism was introduced, not long after Wundt's student, Edward B. Titchener, formally released structuralism to the psychological community. Functionalism was inspired by intellectuals and brilliants minds such as Charles Darwin. Functionalism took structuralism and pushed out the idea of focusing on the elements of a person's consciousness and instead, focused on the individual patient and what differences were accounted for.

- *Behaviorism-* This entity of Psychological frameworks was originally brought forth in 1913, when John B. Watson published, "Psychology as the Behaviorist Views It." Behaviorism is completely and solely based on the outward actions of a person with no focus given on inner thoughts and emotions. Watson, fully encapsulated the idea of behaviorism when he said:

"It is believed that all behaviors are due to the conditioning and education a person received from the moment they were born".

- *Cognitivism-* Cognitivism was created as a response to the rise of behaviorism. Psychologists argued that thought was more than a behavior. They believe that thought is what creates behaviors and therefore can't be one in its own. This theoretical practice studies the ideas, thoughts, processes, and intellect and not the behavior of the individual.

- *Psychoanalysis-* Psychoanalysis is probably the most widely known framework of traditional psychology. This process involves a bit of each type of above, coupled with the effect of childhood experiences and how they relate to the adult process. There is an emphasis on the mental health processes that individuals go through without even knowing that they are.

General Psychological Framework

While all of the above mentioned, are used in some theoretical fashion within psychology, the general framework is more in tune with the specific type of treatment that the patient will undergo. There are four main types.

- • Psychotherapy Within the Humanistic Model

- • Psychotherapy Within the Cognitive Model

- • Psychotherapy Within the Psychodynamic Model

- • Psychotherapy Within the Family Model

All four of these you will find within the mainstream of psychological community. However, when you begin to cross over to Dark Psychology, these things change, and the therapy is less and the research more. Oftentimes, it will take a very specific sector of psychology to dive into the minds of someone blocked by Dark Psychology. There are no real explanations to why these people tend to be more difficult to talk to, but those in the .01 percent rarely react to any of the above therapies.

The Dark Continuum

All individuals have the ability to tap into their dark psyche, but the majorities do only on a very miniscule level. Then there are those criminals that move down the spectrum further and further until the end and they contribute 01 percent of heinous and indescribable crimes. Imagine that the aspects of Dark Psychology sit on a line. Those that use actions that fall under the dark spectrum sit on this line. All deviance, acts of malice, manipulative actions, and perverse behaviors, sit somewhere in the dark line. The dark line is not just specific to action but to feelings, thoughts, ideas, and points of view as well. This line represents all dark psyches within the realm of this sector of dark psychology.

In comparison, you can also picture a Venn diagram where the three circles overlap each other. Within each of the sections of the diagram are the thoughts, actions, etc. Some overlap with each other, while others stand alone. The outer edges of the circle can be interpreted as the less volatile sectors of Dark Psychology, while those intersecting inner circles include, up to, the .01 percent.

While the acts and thoughts within a dark psyche do fall into the diagram or line dependent on their severity, the Continuum is not meant to be a tool used to decide the specific severity of the occurrence. Nuccitelli is currently working further on this concept as it is not complete. Through more research and a more open expansion of studies within Dark Psychology, the Dark Continuum will filter down to a more precise theory.

The Dark Factor

The Dark Factor, while relatively new in the world of psychology, is not something that has been hidden from psychological practice through the years. Charles Spearman, an English psychologist in 1904, made two of the most important discoveries in Psychology till date. The first discovery was based on the idea that there was a general factor of intelligence, the g-factor. This factor defined the rate of scoring for intelligence and founded the fact that regardless of the indicator, as long as the test is thorough and sufficient, you will be able to measure the cognitive intelligence of a person.

Ultimately, Moshagen and his associates have answered the long-standing question of whether there was one force that unified all dark traits. This would be the D-Factor. It shows that there is not just one single trait that defines a dark psyche, but that there is a multitude of human traits, some good, some bad, that culminate into the level of darkness your psyche consists of. When testing their theory, the team used nine different traits, well established within the psychology realm, and tested people on them. The traits used were:

- Spitefulness

- Self-Interest

- Sadism

- Psychopathy

- Psychological Entitlement

- Narcissism

- Moral Disengagement

- Machiavellianism

- Egoism

People from all walks of life were tested and the results were combined and studied. In the end, the team came up with the following conclusions:

1. It was found that there was a positive relation between all of the dark traits tested for.

2. The most relatable D-Factor items fell into patterns that gave a basis for their theory. The theory closely attached the ideas of utility maximization, inflicting disutility, and justifying malevolent beliefs.

3. They found that the people having higher D-Factor scores, when given money, were more likely to keep it to themselves. On top of this finding, these people were also more likely to have unethical behaviors like cheating.

4. The D-Factor was closely related to self-centeredness, dominance, impulsive behaviors, a need for power, aggressive tendencies, and morality issues. At the same time, they were also related to things such as sincere actions, fair ideas, an avoidance to greed, and modest behavior.

5. The D-Factor does not relate to only one measure. Even when tested repeatedly, removing different variables from the experiment, the correlations were the same.

The Dark Factor tests were much more complex than just the above tests. Information about the person's background, family history, temperament, and experiences in life were also taken into account. This test has paved the way for much further research into the dark temperament and has been widely accepted amongst the psychological community. This test should lead the idea of Dark Psychology further into the realm of everyday psychology. One question that is often asked though, is what is at the center of the D-Factor? What type of person is the very darkest, the very center of the flower bud?

This idea is referred to as the Dark Singularity.

The Dark Singularity

Before we dive into the very meaning of Dark Singularity within the realm of Dark Psychology, it is important to note a couple of ideas that will help you further understand the depth that humans are capable of reaching with the Dark Factor. While on the surface of everyday life, we tend to think of negative things as having boundaries or borders.

Our human brains do not like the idea of something being far more evil or ominous than we are capable of comprehending.

Science has a lot of different ideas that the human brain does not have the capacity to fully wrap itself around.

<u>Singularity in General Terms</u>

In science, a singularity is a point in space and time that has an infinite value. It is most often discussed when it comes to the infinite density at the tiny center of a black hole. In theory, the center of a black hole never ends, it is infinite.

Therefore, it is theorized that the force of gravity can compress an object, so far that it just has zero volume and becomes infinitely dense. At this point, the point of singularity is believed that space and time no longer exist on the scale that the human mind recognizes because, space and time are completely different and the laws of physics cannot be applied.

The very magnitude of this type of event is almost impossible for our brains to fully understand. We are surrounded by all of the things that make life possible. Gravity, air, pressure, density, all in perfect symbiotic balance with our human bodies, or vice versa.

To imagine a place in space and time that is so different can be unbelievable and almost frightening.

What people don't realize is that on a smaller scale, a theoretical scale that does not involve being crushed to infinite density, singularity can be applied to these things in our current day and time.

This is where the theory of Dark Singularity comes into play.

Singularity in Dark Psychology

Within the confines of our known universe and beyond, a massive black hole sits in the middle of each galaxy with its whirling, raging, benevolent force, cascading energy inward, taking in everything that comes its way, and giving nothing back, not even a single ray of light. It is one of the most unknown but fantastical aspects about space, even within our own galaxy. Dark Singularity is one and the same. Forget the picture of the flower above and imagine the Dark-Factor as a swirling galaxy. Each and every star, every streak of gas, is a personality trait that humans are capable of having. In the center of that galaxy is nothing but dark. In the center, is the point of singularity.

That point of infinite density represents the most heinous, unbelievably evil person ever to exist. But beyond that, there are no bounds to the evilness that can be found within this swirling darkness. There is no end in sight and no reason or understanding of how they came to be. They are powerful, and often unstoppable, destroying everything that comes near them. They are beyond the worst killers we've ever known, even beyond the deepest imagination of evil that is out there. They have no rhyme or reason for the evil that they do and have no sense of moral or emotion toward it either. They are simply doing what their dark psyche tells them to. That is what Dark Singularity is.

With each Machiavellian act, a person slips closer and closer to the point of infinite density. Though, if you really stop to think about it, if it is infinite, there is no stopping. There is no level in which they hit a wall. The possibilities are endless. However, if you subscribe to the Adlerian theory, there wouldn't be a single person to ever reach the infinite point of density because everyone is born with a purpose. That .01 percent from the 99.9 are those that do not fit beneath the described ideals of Adler. They are the ones with no purpose to their evil.

Most of the theory of Dark Singularity was created by Nuccitelli through his own research and the research performed by Alfred Adler and Carl Jung many years before. Like all other forms of science, we build our theories on the backs of those that have come before. We mold and shape our ideas of the human construct from the experiences we have had, and others have had through the course of time. In theory, the Dark Singularity very much could exist, but if we had always known what was over the event horizon, just beyond that point of singularity, would we believe there was no end to the depths of evil a human being could reach? Maybe it's possible or maybe not. Infinite is just a word created to portray an existence too far and too large to ever know if there is an end.

The .01 percent is the focus of many psychologists and criminologists. They are the most elusive, the least understood, and the most dangerous. There are four types of dark personality traits that are the worst out of all of them. Psychopaths, Narcissists, Machiavellians, and Sadists and they all sit eerily at the dark end of the line. Are you one of these? Let's find out.

Conclusion

While many will assume, they know the dark underbelly of humanity, they do not. They only learn what their own lives have conditioned them to see. They see what their individual histories may dictate they see. They often don't realize that they often see what others want them to see.

We all create an illusion about ourselves, our situations, maybe even our realities. We chose to live in them and portray them as true because it can often make life easier to bear. We do the things we do, not intending on hurting anyone around us. In most cases, you will find that there is usually little to no malice in the words of most people in a civilized society. They go about their business doing the best that they can. Unfortunately, not all of humanity operates like this.

There are people in history, and some living among us today, who seemed to have had a natural proclivity for doing what seems unnatural. They operate in ways that seem to baffle the minds of the rest of the population. They can even do things that can turn the stomachs of many decent people.

In order to help dispel some of the mysteries behind the ways of these people, you were shown how they can be a part of our everyday lives as lawyers, leaders, salesmen, public speakers, celebrities, etc. The essence of their very techniques was gutted and presented to you as honestly as possible. On top of everything you have already learnt dark psychology, you were shown some of the other tactics dark persuaders may use against you in some unexpected settings. This all happened while a clear division between people who use this on purpose and by mistake was maintained as to avoid creating unnecessary suspicion and paranoia, especially in more sensitive readers. The journey would only get darker from there. While you dove into the personality traits of these kinds of people, you were given a lot of insight into what makes people who can be considered as having 'dark personalities' tick. Hopefully, you have gained valuable knowledge regarding how these people may operate. Perhaps you even learned about the best ways to adopt some of these stratagems for your own benefit. How you use them is completely up to you. Manipulation is a necessary evil to learn about as it exists all around us. Learning about this is a natural extension of learning about reading people as the two go hand-in-hand. This is especially true because of all the things you may have found in this book. Reading and manipulation are the only two things everyone does as unconsciously as they draw breath. There is no end to telling how vital this information can be if taken seriously, especially for those who want to have more of a say in the partners they end up with.